WRITE YOUR OWN HOROSCOPE

JANE STRUTHERS

ILLUSTRATIONS BY LAURA MEDLICOTT

WHITE LION
PUBLISHING

To my life-long friend Chris Granville-Edge,
a shining example of a creative and generous Leo, with love

Contents

How to Use This Book

Are you new to astrology? Maybe you already know a little about your star sign (or Sun sign, to be more accurate) but not much more than that. Don't worry, because this how-to horoscope book will help you navigate your way through the complexities of your birth chart, with plenty of key tips and takeaways to keep you on track.

Your chart is a snapshot of the heavens at the very moment you were born, and analyzing it will give you a rich understanding of precisely who you are. You'll be able to examine areas of your personality that have remained a mystery to you until now, as well as gain greater insight into the personalities of your partner, friends and family via their birth charts.

Reading Your Horoscope

This book is called *Write Your Own Horoscope*, but what exactly is a horoscope? Is it your birth chart, or is it a forecast of your future? It's both! This book will show you not only how to interpret your chart, set for the time, date and place you were born, but it will also teach you how to look into your future, so you can see the trends that are coming up for you in the days, weeks, months and years ahead.

Forecasting the Future

You'll learn how to create tailor-made predictions about your future, based on the planets making contact ('transits') with your birth chart. Although you may long to dive straight into this area of the book, your results will be more accurate if you first use *Write Your Own Horoscope* to explore and interpret your chart.

Understanding your birth chart will give you a good idea of how you'll react to the transits coming up for you. That's because a natal planet (a planet in the sign and degree it occupied when we were born) affects us both externally and internally, so the way your best friend reacts to a particular planet may be quite different from your response. To give you an example, if your chart shows that you're shy, sensitive, are happiest at home and that you hesitate to take risks, a transit from Jupiter (the planet of expansion, which includes travel and education) is unlikely to inspire you to splurge on an airline ticket so you can explore a remote part of the world. Instead, you might decide to learn something new at home, or your life might be broadened when you get to know someone from another culture or country.

What Do You Need to Use This Book?

Very little! Armed with your birth details, you can consult a free astrology website, which will calculate your chart. Alternatively, you can invest in an astrology computer program. Then just print out the chart, ready to analyze it with the help of this book. When you want to forecast the future, you can use the website or program to calculate the transits and refer to this book to interpret the results.

Getting It Right

Maybe you're thinking that you could find a website that does all of this for you? The snag is that some sites aren't very accurate, only give sketchy information, or focus on your Sun sign rather than your entire chart. The benefit of this book is that it's crammed with detailed and accurate information, focusing on the most important areas of our lives: love and sex; work and career; money; relationships and family; and how to harness your potential. There are also hints and tips throughout to guide you every step of the way into the fascinating world of astrology.

How to Write Your Own Horoscope

You can write your own horoscope in two ways. The first is to analyze your own birth chart to explore what it reveals about you. The second is to use it to look into your future over different time frames.

Writing a Daily Horoscope

If you want to see what's coming up for you on a specific day, use an astrology program that allows you to select the transits for that particular day. Consider each transit in turn and don't ignore lunar transits because they'll show how you'll be feeling and reacting to what's going on around you.

Writing a Weekly Horoscope

You need to consider every area of your chart affected by transits, so you can get an overall impression of what the week will bring. Note any New or Full Moons because they'll add emotional colour to the week. New Moons signal the start of something new, according to where they fall in your natal chart. Full Moons signify endings.

Writing a Monthly Horoscope

Look more broadly at the transits occurring during this time. Start by interpreting the transits from the slowest-moving planets. Note the sign of the transiting Sun because that will tell you which area of your birth chart is being activated by the Sun's energy.

Writing an Annual Horoscope

You can't possibly interpret every transit during an entire year, so you need to take an overall look at what your future holds. Start by noting any transits from Pluto, Neptune, Uranus, Saturn and Jupiter. These move slowly so create a long-lasting influence. You can also cast a special chart, called a solar return, set for your birthday, that will show you what's coming up over the course of the year.

1

The nuts and bolts of astrology

If you're wondering how astrology works, this chapter will give you a simple explanation. Although you can still write your own horoscope without this knowledge, it will provide a good framework for understanding the roles that the planets and zodiac play in your life.

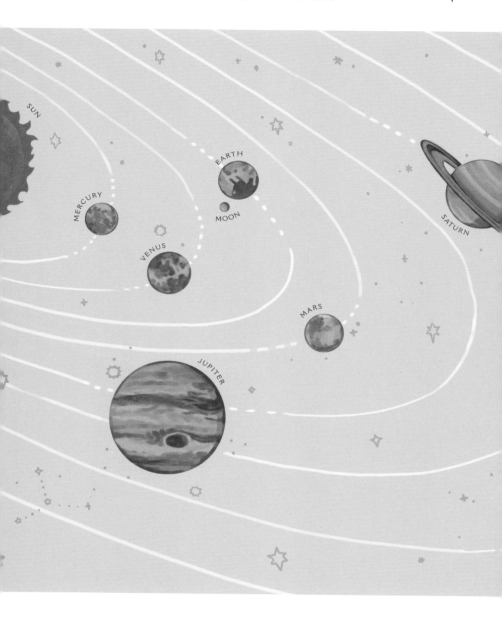

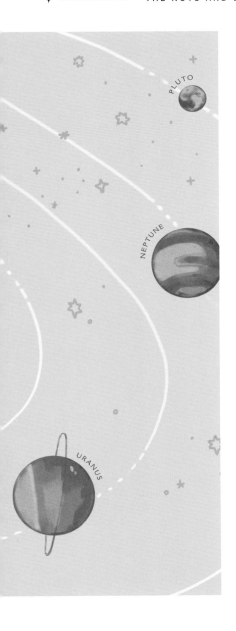

The Solar System

Here we are on Planet Earth, spinning through space, orbiting the centre of our solar system: the Sun. 'Solar' means 'related to the Sun', and the Earth, in common with the other planets, revolves around it.

THE PLANETS

Astrology focuses on the movement of ten planets. You may think there are only seven – Mercury, Venus, Mars, Jupiter, Saturn, Uranus and Neptune – but the Sun and Moon both count as planets in astrology, even though astrologers know that the Sun is a star and the Moon is a satellite of the Earth. And although Pluto was demoted to the status of a dwarf planet by the International Astronomical Union (IAU) in 2006, there's no doubting the fact that he's anything but a dwarf planet when you consider the influence he has on us astrologically.

✦

Although we know that the Earth is a planet, we don't usually include it in an astrology chart because that is set using Earth as our vantage point.

✦

The Zodiac

If you want to understand how astrology works, you need to use your imagination. Picture the Earth, with the Sun and the rest of the planets orbiting around it in a circle that sits at a slight angle to the equator. Now imagine that the backdrop of this circle is a belt of stars, made up of different constellations. As the Sun, Moon and other planets appear to orbit us here on Earth, they look as though they're moving along this starry belt. In astronomy, it's called the ecliptic.

Many centuries ago, astronomers divided the ecliptic into twelve equal sections of 30 degrees and named each one after the constellation that was nearest to it. These constellations gave their names to the twelve zodiac signs that we know today, although they don't fit neatly into these twelve divisions: Aries, Taurus, Gemini, Cancer, Leo, Virgo, Libra, Scorpio, Sagittarius, Capricorn, Aquarius and Pisces.

Think of these zodiac signs as the celestial backdrop to the movements of the planets. Each sign is associated with a particular animal, human or object, because of the mythology surrounding its constellation. You might think that these associations are just ancient legends, but they tell us a great deal about the characteristics of each zodiac sign. For instance, Taurus is the sign of the Bull, and Taureans can sometimes show all the obstinacy of a bull.

In astrology, each sign is associated with a particular planet. That planet is called the sign's ruler and has a major influence on the way the sign behaves. Let's take Aries as an example. It's ruled by Mars, known as the fiery planet, and Aries is renowned for its equally fiery temperament.

Scorpio, Aquarius and Pisces have two planetary rulers each. The first is the traditional ruler; the second is the modern ruler. Uranus was discovered in 1781, Neptune in 1846 and Pluto in 1930, and they were given rulership of the signs that closely matched their characteristics. Some astrologers only use the traditional rulers.

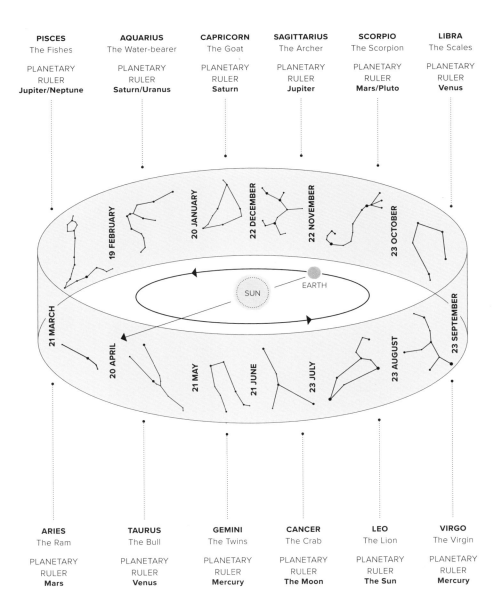

PISCES
The Fishes

PLANETARY
RULER
Jupiter/Neptune

AQUARIUS
The Water-bearer

PLANETARY
RULER
Saturn/Uranus

CAPRICORN
The Goat

PLANETARY
RULER
Saturn

SAGITTARIUS
The Archer

PLANETARY
RULER
Jupiter

SCORPIO
The Scorpion

PLANETARY
RULER
Mars/Pluto

LIBRA
The Scales

PLANETARY
RULER
Venus

19 FEBRUARY
20 JANUARY
22 DECEMBER
22 NOVEMBER
23 OCTOBER

21 MARCH

SUN
EARTH

23 SEPTEMBER

20 APRIL
21 MAY
21 JUNE
23 JULY
23 AUGUST

ARIES
The Ram

PLANETARY
RULER
Mars

TAURUS
The Bull

PLANETARY
RULER
Venus

GEMINI
The Twins

PLANETARY
RULER
Mercury

CANCER
The Crab

PLANETARY
RULER
The Moon

LEO
The Lion

PLANETARY
RULER
The Sun

VIRGO
The Virgin

PLANETARY
RULER
Mercury

Astrology and the Planets

The planets are rich in meaning, mythology and symbolism. Here's a short introduction to the astrological significance of each one, and the different characteristics they represent.

The Sun

Identity; sense of self; heroic journey through life; what makes you tick; what lights you up; father figures

The Moon

Instincts; habits; knee-jerk reactions; what feels familiar; home; family; needs; what feeds you literally and emotionally; mother figures

Mercury

The way you think and what you think about; powers of communication; siblings; negotiations; versatility; youth

Venus

Emotions; love; ability to love and be loved; what you enjoy; what you yearn for; your fashion sense; money; what makes you happy

Mars

Drive and motivation; determination; what you want and how you get it; anger; aggression; sex; strength

♃
Jupiter

Luck; optimism; positivity;
expansion; growth;
abundance; confidence;
travel; wisdom; beliefs; higher
education; generosity

Uranus, Neptune and Pluto are collectively known as
the outer planets. They are so far away from the Sun
that they have a huge orbit, so from our perspective
on Earth they move very slowly and take a long time
to pass through each zodiac sign. This means that
Neptune and Pluto, in particular, have more of a
generational influence on you than a personal one,
unless they form aspects to your Sun, Moon, Mercury,
Venus or Mars, or, to a lesser extent, Jupiter or Saturn.

♅
Uranus

Eccentricity; genius;
surprises; shocks;
breaking the rules;
turning things on their
head; being ahead
of your time; friendly
actions; humanitarian

♄
Saturn

Authority; restrictions; delays;
pessimism; responsibilities;
age; slowness; common
sense; tenacity; foundations;
structure; father figures

♆
Neptune

Mysticism; spirituality;
refinement of all
kinds; confusion;
romance; imagination;
sensitivity; altruism;
being charitable;
being self-defeating

♇
Pluto

Profound change; confronting taboos;
uncovering buried treasure; survival;
eliminating what is no longer needed

The Twelve Signs

Each zodiac sign has its own particular set of
characteristics, as described opposite. If you're
only used to the idea of your Sun being in a
particular sign – this is often referred to as your
star sign, although it should really be known
as your Sun sign, because it's the sign that the
Sun occupied when you were born – you now
need to expand that thought to encompass the
knowledge that each of the nine other planets
falls in a specific zodiac sign as well. Your birth
chart contains all twelve signs, although you
won't have a planet in each of them.

ARIES
Adventurous; daring; enthusiastic; great at starting things but bad at finishing them; 'me first' attitude; pioneering; impatient

TAURUS
Steady; pragmatic; practical; grounded; possessive; materialistic; sensual; determined; strong-willed; stubborn; strong ideas

GEMINI
Versatile; flexible; fickle; flirtatious; quick-witted; bright; easily bored; chatty; enjoys being busy; has many interests

CANCER
Sentimental; emotional; intuitive; imaginative; moody; touchy and huffy; family-minded; likes tradition; nostalgic; defensive; tends to worry

LEO
Regal; dignified; snobbish; strong need for self-expression; loving; generous; protective of others; organizational skills; self-important

VIRGO
Fastidious; practical; tidy; reliable; likes to be of service to others; anxious; nervy; fussy; modest; discriminating; interested in health

LIBRA
Tactful; charming; considerate; need for balance and harmony; needs to be liked and loved; indecisive; can see both sides of every argument

SCORPIO
Strong emotions; willpower; self-control; still waters run deep; dogmatic; jealous; controlling; passionate; intense; secretive

SAGITTARIUS
Open-minded; curious; jovial; gregarious; optimistic; tactless; blunt; freedom-loving; restless; enthusiastic; generous

CAPRICORN
Careful; cautious; reserved; shy; likes convention; hard-working; ambitious; dependable; disciplined; prudent; stoic

AQUARIUS
Independent; idiosyncratic; original; unusual; idealistic; reforming zeal; gift for friendship; opinionated; inflexible

PISCES
Sensitive emotions; romantic; intuitive; compassionate; empathic; kind; takes the line of least resistance; easily swayed by others

Goals; responsibilities; your public image; your dominant parent

Expansion; exploration; long-distance travel; foreigners; higher education; beliefs

Friends; group activities; teamwork; societies; hobbies; long-term hopes and wishes

Intimate relationships; sex; death; taboo topics; shared finances; insurance; tax

Your hidden self; institutions; charities; self-sacrifice; self-sabotage

One-to-one relationships of all kinds; open enemies; legal matters

Your physical appearance and body; how you view the world

Being of service; duty; your health; your daily routine; day-to-day work; colleagues; pets

Your values; your personal finances; what you buy; possessions; assets

Creativity; self-expression; fun; children; competitiveness; love; drama; gambling

Communications; short journeys; siblings; neighbours; cars, bicycles; schools

The home; family and domestic life; the past; endings; your less dominant parent

12 11 10 9 8 7 6 5 4 3 2 1

The Twelve Houses

Every horoscope is divided into twelve sections, known as houses, and the planets sit within them. Each house rules a different area of life. The art of astrology is to marry the meaning of the planet and the sign it occupies with the arena of life that's described by the house it falls in. Combining these takes practice, so be patient if it takes a while to master it.

After you've read the meaning of each house, pair them up by comparing the 1st with the 7th, the 2nd with the 8th, the 3rd with the 9th, and so on. You will see how they balance each other. For instance, the 1st house is about 'me' and the 7th house, which deals with relationships, is about 'we'.

HOUSE SYSTEMS

If you're using a computer program to calculate a chart, you'll be asked to choose a house system. Start off with a popular system such as Equal House or Placidus. Equal House is just that – each house contains an equal number of degrees. More complex systems also exist, such as Placidus, using houses of different sizes.

The Four Angles

We've seen how a birth chart is divided into twelve houses. But it is also divided into four quadrants by what are known as the angles, and these have a very important role in astrology.

The four angles operate in pairs that are each separated by 180 degrees:

*   The Ascendant–Descendant axis

*   The MC–IC axis

To put it very simply, the angles refer to the points of a compass. However, it's a compass that has been turned upside down, to reflect the clockwise movement of the planets. Every planet rises in the east as it crosses the Ascendant (the left-hand angle at 9 o'clock), reaches its highest point in the south (the top angle at 12 o'clock), sets in the west (the right-hand angle at 3 o'clock) and reaches its lowest point in the north (the bottom angle at 6 o'clock). Note that the signs run around the birth chart in an anti-clockwise direction.

WHAT THE ANGLES MEAN

Each set of angles runs on an axis, so any planet in contact with one angle will also be in contact with the angle at the other end of the axis. This means that you need to consider both ends of the axis, such as the MC and the IC. When analyzing an angle you must take into account the sign it occupies as well as any planets contacting it by aspect.

POSITIONS OF THE PLANETS

☉	Sun	15°00'	Taurus
☽	Moon	22°26'	Cancer
☿	Mercury	3°06'	Gemini
♀	Venus	3°15'	Taurus
♂	Mars	23°53'	Cancer
♃	Jupiter	9°27'	Taurus
♄	Saturn	27°20'	Cancer
♅	Uranus	4°41'	Scorpio
♆	Neptune	13°20'	Sagittarius
♇	Pluto	9°26'	Libra
	Ascendant	2°58'	Aries
	Descendant	2°58'	Libra
	MC	1°52'	Capricorn
	IC	1°52'	Cancer

THE MC

This is what you're aiming at in life, and it describes your public persona. For this reason it's considered of great importance when assessing your career and professional life.

THE DESCENDANT

This shows the way you connect with other people, as well as the style of relationships you're most comfortable with.

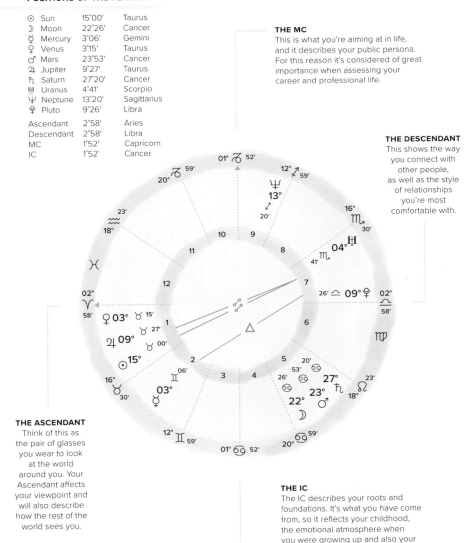

THE ASCENDANT

Think of this as the pair of glasses you wear to look at the world around you. Your Ascendant affects your viewpoint and will also describe how the rest of the world sees you.

THE IC

The IC describes your roots and foundations. It's what you have come from, so it reflects your childhood, the emotional atmosphere when you were growing up and also your ancestral roots.

The Five Major Aspects

Whenever two planets are within a specific number of degrees of each other in a chart, they are said to form an aspect. This means they give the other planet some of their energy, which affects how each of them operates. They're in contact with each other, but what is that contact like? Are they doing the planetary equivalent of holding hands so their energies flow, or are they squaring up for a fight? That depends on the particular aspect.

Throughout this book you'll see descriptions of what happens when each planet forms an aspect to another planet. To understand a specific aspect, all you need do is blend your knowledge of the combination of planets with your understanding of each aspect.

THE BIG FIVE

We're going to concentrate on the five major planetary aspects, although if you study astrology in more depth you'll discover that there are several so-called minor aspects too. In the charts shown, you'll see how each of these five major aspects works, and also how many degrees separate them. Each aspect is allowed an 'orb' – a number of degrees either side of exactitude. Generally speaking, the more exact an aspect is, the more instinctively a person expresses the energies of that aspect. The wider the orb, the more conscious the person is of those energies, so if they aren't helpful, the person may have more control over them.

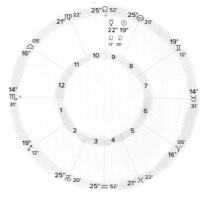

Conjunction ☌
Exact 0˚, Orb 8˚
The energies of the two planets are combined. Conjunctions are always an important area in a chart because they're the focus of so much energy, especially if more than two planets are involved. With three or more planets in a conjunction, you must analyze each pair separately so you can build up a complete picture of how they all work together.

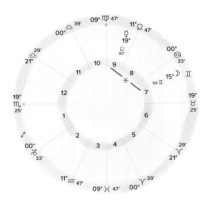

Sextile ✶
Exact 60°, Orb 4°
An easy-going aspect in which the two planets help each other and can create opportunities, but some effort is needed to get the best out of them.

Square ☐
Exact 90°, Orb 8°
Tension! These planets are at right angles to each other, so it can feel as though the energies clash and there is no way forward. However, squares offer great scope for personal growth and self-knowledge.

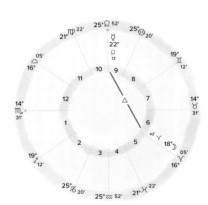

Trine △
Exact 120°, Orb 6°
The energies of the two planets flow freely, which can be great if they bring positive action but is more challenging if they encourage negative activities or attitudes.

Opposition ☍
Exact 180°, Orb 8°
Two opposing forces trying to come together and balance one another. Very often an opposition is most active in our relationships when we project our problems or potentials on to others rather than owning them ourselves.

The Four Elements and Three Modes

There are two more factors to consider when analyzing your chart: the elements and the modes. The specific balance of elements and modes will provide further important information about yourself. Do you like to get things done? Do you prefer to take a more passive approach? Are you optimistic? Do you focus on the practical side of life, worrying about the details, or do you have a more happy-go-lucky attitude?

THE ELEMENTS

In the West, we believe that the natural world is composed of four elements: fire, earth, air and water. These four elements are very important astrologically because they describe specific ways of behaving and connecting with the world around us. Each of the twelve signs belongs to one of these four elements, making three signs in each element. When you add up the number of signs in each element in a chart you'll discover whether one or more of them is emphasized or lacking. This immediately gives you some fundamental information about that person's character.

Enthusiastic; warm; active; takes the initiative; optimistic; idealistic; inspired

Fire

Aries
Leo
Sagittarius

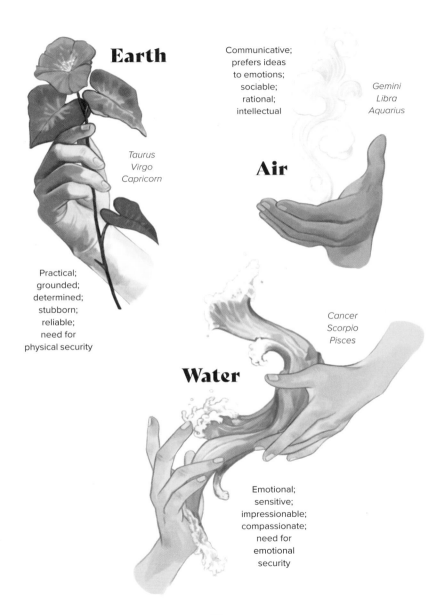

Earth

*Taurus
Virgo
Capricorn*

Practical;
grounded;
determined;
stubborn;
reliable;
need for
physical security

Communicative;
prefers ideas
to emotions;
sociable;
rational;
intellectual

*Gemini
Libra
Aquarius*

Air

*Cancer
Scorpio
Pisces*

Water

Emotional;
sensitive;
impressionable;
compassionate;
need for
emotional
security

THE MODES

As well as dividing the signs into elements, we also divide them into three different modes: cardinal, fixed and mutable. These describe our approach to life — for instance, whether we get on with things single-mindedly or have a more fluid attitude.

CARDINAL Aries, Cancer, Libra, Capricorn	FIXED Taurus, Leo, Scorpio, Aquarius	MUTABLE Gemini, Virgo, Sagittarius, Pisces
Motivated; dynamic; good at starting things; driven; ambitious	Excellent staying power; likes to maintain the status quo; lacks flexibility	Flexible and versatile; restless; needs change; can be wary of commitment

PUTTING THE ELEMENTS AND MODES TOGETHER

Each of the twelve signs has a different combination of element and mode. Here they are so you can see them at a glance.

	FIRE	EARTH	AIR	WATER
CARDINAL	Aries	Capricorn	Libra	Cancer
FIXED	Leo	Taurus	Aquarius	Scorpio
MUTABLE	Sagittarius	Virgo	Gemini	Pisces

WORKING IT OUT

Here's how you do it, using a sample chart. Don't include the planets Uranus, Neptune and Pluto because they are so impersonal. Allow two counts for the Sun and Moon, and one count for Mercury to Saturn, plus the Ascendant and MC.

	FIRE	EARTH	AIR	WATER	MODES TOTAL
CARDINAL		Ascendant (1)	Sun (2) Mercury (1)		4
FIXED	Moon (2)			Venus (1) Mars (1) MC (1)	5
MUTABLE	Jupiter (1)			Saturn (1)	2
ELEMENTS TOTAL	3	1	3	4	

In the Modes Totals, fixed scores highest (5), while water scores highest (4) in the Elements Totals. This means an emphasis on fixed and water signs, as well as a Scorpio (fixed water) flavour to Chloe's chart. With only the Ascendant in earth, she is lacking in this element and may try to compensate by being extra grounded and practical, or attracting others like this.

Putting It All Together

If you haven't interpreted your birth chart before, don't worry if you're feeling a bit daunted. It's quite natural. After all, there is a lot to take in and remember — although of course you don't have to remember it all at once.

At the moment we're looking at analyzing the birth chart, not forecasting what's coming up for you, because if you don't understand your chart first, you won't be able to properly interpret what the future holds. Chapter 7 is your guide to mapping your future, but in the meantime, as you work through each chapter you'll see plenty of hints and tips about forecasting, which you can refer to whenever you want to look at what the days, weeks, months or years ahead hold for you.

KEEP IT SIMPLE!

The key to successful astrological interpretation is to keep it simple and look at each factor in turn:

* The balance of elements in the chart
* The balance of modes in the chart
* The distribution of planets around the chart
* The sign that each planet falls in
* The house that each planet occupies
* The angles of the chart
* The aspects and angles that the planets form with each other
* Any planets that don't aspect other planets

Do this systematically, otherwise you'll end up in a terrible muddle. It helps to write your findings in a notebook rather than on your phone or computer, because writing by hand helps your intuition and ideas to flow. What's more, you can illustrate your notes or highlight anything that jumps out at you, or sketch and annotate your chart, and it means you've got all your thoughts in one place.

ORDERING YOUR THOUGHTS

Once you've looked at all the factors listed opposite, it's up to you to choose the order in which you analyze them, although the most logical way is to use the order given. Start with the central themes that colour the chart: the balance of elements and modes, followed by the distribution of the planets – are they grouped together in clusters, are they spread out, are any of them separated from the rest of the planets? Even this simple analysis will give you some valuable information, such as whether there's an emphasis on a particular element or sign, or the fact that three planets are tightly grouped together in one section of the chart. After that, you can analyze each planet individually, gathering all the information you can find on it before moving on to the next. Work slowly and carefully through each astrological factor, ending with any planets that are unaspected, until you've built up a good picture of the owner of the chart.

Your birth chart is a snapshot of the heavens at the moment you were born. But the planets keep moving, and as they do they make contact with your birth chart. These are called transits – the planet is transiting your chart. It will help to remember this term when reading the information about forecasting in the following chapters.

Analyzing Your Chart

Now that we've covered the theory about how to analyze a birth chart, let's do it for real, so you can see how it all works.

Olivia
Natal
20 Sep 1998, Sun
1:18 PM BST -1:00
London, England
Tropical
Placidus

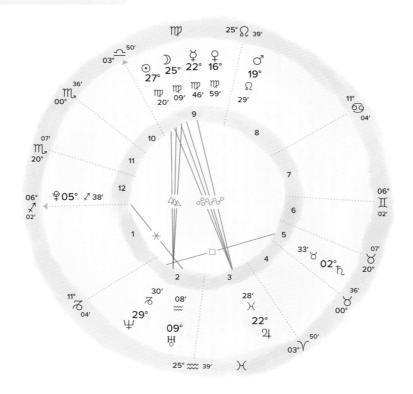

Start with the balance of elements and modes.

	FIRE	EARTH	AIR	WATER	MODES TOTAL
CARDINAL			MC (1)		1
FIXED	Mars (1)	Saturn (1)			2
MUTABLE	Ascendant (1)	Sun (2) Moon (2) Mercury (1) Venus (1)		Jupiter (1)	8
ELEMENTS TOTAL	2	7	1	1	

There is a planet or angle in every element and mode, but they are out of balance, with a great emphasis on the earth element and the mutable mode. This gives the chart a powerful Virgo flavour (mutable earth), which will strengthen Olivia's Sun and Moon in Virgo.

How are the planets distributed around the chart? Look at the group of four planets (Venus, Mercury, Moon and Sun) in Virgo in the 9th house. This is a powerful concentration of energy, and it gets further impetus from the Sun's conjunction with the Libra MC. Pluto is sitting on the Sagittarius Ascendant, and Neptune and Uranus are in the 2nd house but are too far apart to be conjunct.

There aren't many aspects to analyze, but just look at Jupiter in Pisces in the 3rd house. It's forming an opposition to the group (known as a stellium) in the 9th house, which adds even more emphasis to it. Are any planets unaspected? Yes – Mars in Leo in the 8th. This tells us that Mars is doing its own thing here, unaffected by the other planets and angles.

Already, even without analyzing every factor in the chart, we can see that the main focus in Olivia's chart is the Virgo stellium, opposed by Jupiter (the ruler of the chart, because it rules the Sagittarian Ascendant, thereby giving it extra significance and power). Virgo is a modest sign, needing to express itself in practical and organized ways. It's often uncomfortable being in the limelight or receiving too much attention, yet Olivia's Virgo Sun is in conjunction with the MC, meaning that she enjoys being in the spotlight. Also, the opposition from Jupiter, which tends to expand whatever it contacts, can encourage a strong sense of ego, which of course is the complete opposite of shy Virgo. What's more, Pluto on the Ascendant denotes someone with a powerful personality. So we have some interesting contradictions here — something that often occurs in astrology.

We'd have to ask Olivia exactly how this plays out in her life, but one option is that she has a job connected with travel, higher education or religion (all 9th house areas) in which she helps others (Virgo) and encourages and talks to them (Jupiter in the 3rd house) in some way. Maybe she's a travel rep or a pilot, or perhaps she's a university lecturer who loves chatting to her students, or maybe she writes (Jupiter in the 3rd house) about travel or some other 9th house topic.

There is plenty more to explore in this chart, but already we can see a vivid picture of Olivia emerging.

Taking It One Step Further

We're going to look at a more advanced technique now, so if you're a complete beginner you may not want to explore this until you feel more confident about your astrological knowledge and abilities. But once you know your way around a chart and have a good feel for the meanings of the planets, signs and houses, there's nothing to stop you trying this out. As ever, it's probably best to begin with your own chart because you can then apply your knowledge of astrology to your knowledge of yourself.

THE CUSPS OF THE HOUSES

As you know, there are twelve houses in an astrological chart, each ruling a different area of life. Here's a quick reminder of what they are:

HOUSE	AREA OF LIFE	HOUSE	AREA OF LIFE
1ST	You; your personality; your appearance	7TH	One-to-one relationships; open enemies
2ND	Your values and priorities	8TH	Close relationships; shared values
3RD	Siblings; neighbours; short journeys	9TH	Expansion; long-distance travel
4TH	Home; family; the past; endings	10TH	Ambitions; goals; being in the public eye
5TH	Love; enjoyment; creativity; children	11TH	Friendships; hopes and wishes; hobbies
6TH	Health; work; daily routine	12TH	Privacy; secret enemies

A birth chart contains ten planets and twelve houses, so there is no way that a planet can fall in each house. This can cause a few astrological conundrums at first. For instance, Jacob's chart opposite has no planets in his fifth house. Does this mean he has no love in his life, isn't creative or will never have children? No! It simply means that you will have to look a little deeper into his chart to discover how to express the energies of the 5th house. And the way to do that is to look at the sign on the cusp of that house.

FINDING A CUSP

The cusp of a house is the point where the previous house ends and the new one starts. Different astrology programs show this in different ways, but the number of the house is usually marked in the inner ring of the chart. Find the number of the house you want, then look at the outer ring, showing the signs, to see in which sign the house begins. This will be the sign that influences that house. For instance, Aries on the cusp of the 5th house means that Jacob's style of creativity (5th house) is enthusiastic and lively, and may start quickly but fizzle out if they get bored (Aries). What seemed to be an 'empty' house has now become much more interesting.

Jacob
Natal
13 June 1967, Tue
19:10 BST -1:00
London, United Kingdom
Geocentric
Tropical
Campanus

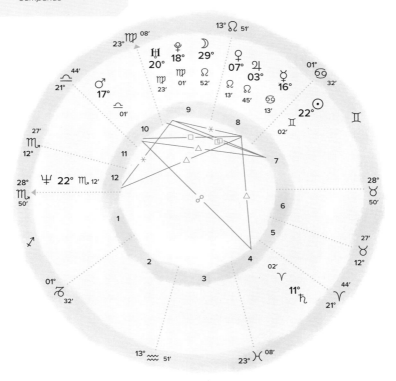

Love and sex

We all need to know we're loved. Of course,
love comes in many forms, but romantic love
is often at the top of the most-wanted list, so
that's what we're exploring in this chapter. We'll
be looking at four planets that have a huge
impact on our attitude to love and sex,
and influence the sort of partners we
attract instinctively. You will learn about
your emotional needs by analyzing
your own horoscope, and with your
partner's date of birth you can
discover their style of loving too.

Astrology and Love

Of all areas of life, relationships can leave us feeling the most vulnerable because they are where we open up emotionally and form a strong bond with others. However, if you want to be a successful astrologer you must realize that your own style of loving isn't the only game in town. We all have our own set of needs, depending on our horoscope, so what's good for us may not be so great for a prospective partner.

Some people put themselves on the line, becoming so dependent on the special person in their life that they feel at their mercy. And when it comes to intimate relationships involving romantic love and sex, we bare all in more ways than one. We can feel powerless and vulnerable, reliant on our beloved to treat us kindly. If they reject us, we collapse, thinking that we can't survive without them.

However, not everyone shares these feelings. Some people are much more self-reliant and resilient, happy to have someone special in their life without being utterly dependent on them. And some might even prefer to be alone, because they're just happier that way. Maybe they don't need other people all that much, or perhaps feel that's the best way to avoid the emotional risks involved in forming close relationships.

LOOKING AT LOVE AND SEX

In this chapter we're looking at four planets that have a big influence on our emotional lives, our capacity to give and receive love, and our desire for sex.

Venus and Mars are intricately bound up with love and sex respectively, and they can't be ignored. But they aren't the whole story. Uranus adds sparkle and electricity – the magical snap, crackle and pop that you feel when you meet someone who makes you light up – and it also governs our need for independence and detachment. Neptune is all about romance and our urge to merge with another, which can be a wonderfully spiritual experience, or can mean we lose our identity and become drawn into a completely symbiotic relationship that doesn't do us any good.

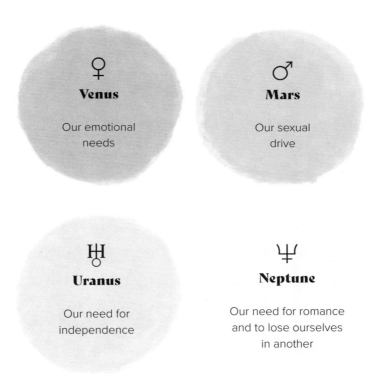

♀
Venus

Our emotional
needs

♂
Mars

Our sexual
drive

♅
Uranus

Our need for
independence

♆
Neptune

Our need for romance
and to lose ourselves
in another

As you will discover, Uranus and Neptune operate slightly differently from Venus and Mars because they are generational planets rather than personal ones. Even so, an aspect between Venus and/or Mars and Uranus and/or Neptune will still have a big impact on the way you experience love and sex. And that goes for your partner too, so when you've finished analyzing your chart, why not look at theirs?

This section looks at Venus in your birth chart, but
you can also use it when forecasting your future. Use an
astrology program to discover which sign Venus is moving
through during the coming month, then refer to the charts to
see how it will influence you emotionally.

Your Venus Sign and Your Style of Love

Want to know about your particular style
of loving and what you yearn for romantically?
Venus, the planet of love, will tell you. The first
step is to consult your birth chart to see which
sign Venus occupied when you were born, and
the second is to use the information in this book
to help you understand how you express love
and affection, and what sort of partner you're
looking for. It's invaluable knowledge!

Check when transiting Venus will be returning to
its natal sign. For instance, if you were born with Venus in
Libra, find out when transiting Venus will next be in Libra.
This will be a time of renewed emotional energy and
a new phase in your relationships.

♀ VENUS IN	YOU NEED	IDEAL PARTNER	CONTROL YOUR
ARIES ♈	Passion, excitement, the thrill of the chase; a new conquest if things get boring	Romantic, sexy, loving; knows how to keep you interested and flattered	Tendency to put yourself first emotionally; idealism
TAURUS ♉	Emotional security; a safe haven; long-term commitment	Dependable; steady; loyal; sensual and affectionate	Tendency to be possessive and stubborn
GEMINI ♊	Light-hearted love; excitement and versatility; the freedom to do your own thing when you wish	Quick-witted; lively; your intellectual match; easy-going	Flirtatious nature if it upsets your partner; your emotional wanderlust
CANCER ♋	To feel loved and needed; safe; emotional stability; someone to love and nurture	Reliable; kind; understanding when you get moody; cuddly	Tendency to sulk or get moody when you feel rejected; tendency to smother-love
LEO ♌	To be appreciated and admired; to let your love flow freely; to show your support and loyalty	Someone you can be proud of; loving; passionate; encouraging; a good audience	Bossiness; need for drama and to be centre-stage
VIRGO ♍	Kindness and consideration; someone who'll listen to your worries; mental freedom	Relaxed, reassuring and stable; neat and tidy	Tendency to nit-pick and find fault with your partner over the smallest things

♀ VENUS IN	YOU NEED	IDEAL PARTNER	CONTROL YOUR
LIBRA ♎	To immerse yourself in close relationships; to be one half of a couple; to soak up compliments	Loving; clever; admiring; attractive; well groomed; considerate	Need to be in love with love; tendency to put partners on pedestals; reluctance to end a relationship for fear of being alone
SCORPIO ♏	Emotional intensity; to feel needed and wanted; passion and sexual fizz; to be transformed by love and sex	Someone who isn't fazed by your intensity and powerful emotions	Jealousy and suspicion; need to control the relationship
SAGITTARIUS ♐	Emotional independence – you can't bear to feel your wings are being clipped; love and support	Funny; generous; gregarious; interested in everything that life has to offer; clever and lively	Need to disappear when the fancy takes you; need to always be right
CAPRICORN ♑	Respect from your partner, especially if you've made sacrifices on their behalf; to provide for your partner if necessary	Understands your need to withdraw emotionally; encourages you to be more demonstrative and openly affectionate	Chilly attitude to love whenever you feel vulnerable or scared of rejection
AQUARIUS ♒	Emotional freedom, without being tied down or expected to behave in ways that don't come naturally to you	Intellectual, able to hold their own in discussions; appreciates your love of friends and isn't threatened by them	Emotional detachment if it drives a wedge between you and your partner; obstinacy
PISCES ♓	Compassion; gentle treatment; loving kindness; someone you can adore and who adores you in return	Empathizes with you but also encourages you to be strong; grounds you and makes you laugh	Emotions whenever they threaten to swamp you; longing for happy-ever-after romance

Venus in the Twelve Houses

Your Venus not only falls in one of the twelve signs of the zodiac, but also in one of the twelve houses, as you will see from your birth chart. The house that your Venus occupies describes the areas of life that you love, as well as good places to meet a partner.

✦

Keep track of Venus as it transits through each house in your birth chart. It will tell you what sort of emotional backdrop to expect at any time. For example, when Venus moves into your 12th house, you'll know that your emotional sensitivity will increase, so you may be more easily hurt, but you'll also be able to tune into others at a deeper and more instinctive level.

✦

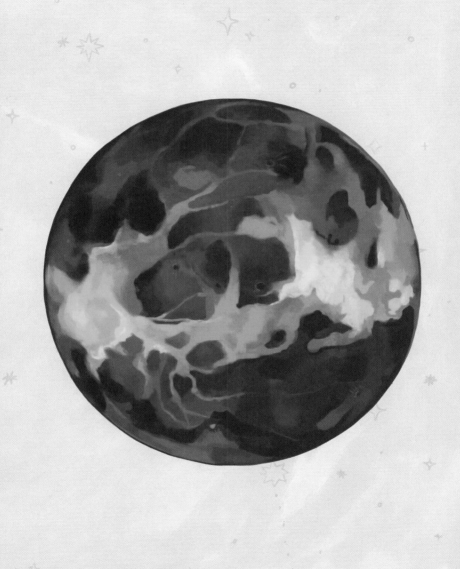

VENUS IN THE TWELVE HOUSES

EMPHASIS ON
Taking care of your partner,
especially materially; creating and
maintaining a good impression

POTENTIAL PITFALLS
Letting your responsibilities
overshadow your relationships;
attracted to someone because of
what they are, not who they are

EMPHASIS ON
Having a partner who is a
friend as well as a lover; enjoying
your social life to the max

POTENTIAL PITFALLS
Spending too much time on
your social life and not enough
on your partner; wary
of commitment

**PLACES TO
MEET A PARTNER**
While pursuing a
goal or ambition;
at work

**PLACES TO
MEET A PARTNER**
Through a hobby or
pastime; with friends;
at a club or society

EMPHASIS ON
Doing your best to be
liked; keeping emotional
secrets; having some
time to yourself

POTENTIAL PITFALLS
Secretly wanting to be
loved and admired;
feeling guilty about
satisfying your
emotional needs

**PLACES TO MEET
A PARTNER**
Through a charity or while
doing volunteer work; in a
hospital or care home

EMPHASIS ON
Your appearance; tact;
charm; pleasing others;
enjoying a busy social life

POTENTIAL PITFALLS
Valuing people and things
according to the way they
look; putting your partner
first then resenting it

**PLACES TO MEET
A PARTNER**
Socially; at a beauty
salon or hairdresser's

**PLACES TO
MEET A PARTNER**
When sorting out
finances; in an
art gallery

**PLACES
TO MEET A
PARTNER**
In your local
area; on a short
journey; through
social media

EMPHASIS ON
Your possessions and values;
the things and people
that make you happy

POTENTIAL PITFALLS
Being too possessive
of others; expecting lavish
gifts from lovers

EMPHASIS ON
Enjoyable conversations; charm
and personality; putting your
feelings into words

POTENTIAL PITFALLS
Being too flirty; always on the
move; having more than one string
to your emotional bow

10
11
12
1
2
3

EMPHASIS ON
Being a free spirit; getting the most out of life, through travel and further education; adventure

POTENTIAL PITFALLS
Never wanting to settle down; always having one eye on the next possible relationship

PLACES TO MEET A PARTNER
On a plane or long-distance journey; on holiday; at university

EMPHASIS ON
Creating a satisfying and intense sexual relationship; connecting at a soul level

POTENTIAL PITFALLS
Unconsciously creating dramas; pent-up jealousy leading to resentment

PLACES TO MEET A PARTNER
In a bank/building society; when sorting out taxes/inheritance

EMPHASIS ON
Happy and fulfilling relationships; creating a long-lasting and loving partnership

PLACES TO MEET A PARTNER
Through a dating agency; in a solicitor's office or in court

POTENTIAL PITFALLS
Wanting to keep the peace at all costs; not ending a relationship even though it's over

PLACES TO MEET A PARTNER
At work; at the doctor's or alternative practitioner's

EMPHASIS ON
Looking after others; ensuring your working conditions are enjoyable and attractive; getting on with colleagues

POTENTIAL PITFALLS
Putting yourself second too often; struggling to cope with people you don't like

PLACES TO MEET A PARTNER
During a celebration; at a wedding; at a betting shop

PLACES TO MEET A PARTNER
At a party in your home; in a shop selling furniture or soft furnishings

EMPHASIS ON
Being fabulous and creating a wonderful impression; lavishing love on others

POTENTIAL PITFALLS
Over-the-top idealism leading to broken dreams; playing the field for too long

EMPHASIS ON
Creating a happy and harmonious home life; gathering loved ones around you and caring for them

POTENTIAL PITFALLS
Feeling hurt if a partner needs their own space; clinging to overly sentimental memories

9 8 7 6 5 4

The tighter the aspect (in other words, the smaller the orb), the more instinctively you'll express its energy, sometimes without even being aware of what you're doing. The wider the aspect, the more self-awareness you'll have about it, giving you more control.

Aspects of Venus – Love

Venus isn't just in a specific sign and house in your chart. It probably also makes one or more aspects to other planets (although in some charts it won't). Remember, aspects are formed when planets are separated by a specific number of degrees – see pages 24–5. Each aspect has an allowable orb because the two planets involved aren't always the exact number of degrees apart. Here is what it means when your Venus forms an aspect to another planet.

INSTANT REMINDER

Conjunction	0°, 8° orb	Energy of the planets is blended
Sextile	60°, 4° orb	Easy-going; opportunities
Square	90°, 8° orb	Tension; trigger for personal growth
Trine	120°, 6° orb	Free-flowing energy
Opposition	180°, 8° orb	Need for balance between opposing forces

VENUS ASPECT	INFLUENCE	STRENGTHENED BY
☉ SUN	Warm; courteous; charming; creative; a need to be liked; can be self-indulgent	Sun in Taurus, Leo or Libra Sun in 2nd, 5th or 7th house Venus in Leo Venus in 5th house
☽ MOON	Loving; affectionate; a need for love and consideration; a need to express emotion; generous	Moon in Taurus, Cancer or Libra Moon in 2nd, 4th or 7th house Venus in 4th house Venus in Cancer
☿ MERCURY	Enjoys putting feelings into words; considerate and diplomatic; good at making romantic gestures	Mercury in Taurus or Libra Mercury in 2nd or 7th house Venus in Gemini or Virgo Venus in 3rd or 6th house
♂ MARS	Sparky; sexy; feisty; enjoys sparring or arguing with a partner and then passionate making up; lively sex life	Mars in Taurus or Libra Mars in 2nd or 7th house Venus in Aries or Scorpio Venus in 1st or 8th house
♃ JUPITER	Generous and affectionate; loves having a good time; popular and gregarious; can struggle with emotional commitment	Jupiter in Taurus or Libra Jupiter in 2nd or 7th house Venus in Sagittarius Venus in 9th house
♄ SATURN	Emotions tempered by self-restraint or shyness; frightened of being hurt; loyal and dependable with the right person	Saturn in Taurus or Libra Saturn in 2nd or 7th house Venus in Capricorn Venus in 10th house
♅ URANUS	Love life can be unpredictable, thanks to a need for excitement; a love of independence can cause problems	Uranus in Taurus or Libra Uranus in 2nd or 7th house Venus in Aquarius Venus in 11th house
♆ NEPTUNE	Emotionally sensitive, with a yearning for happy endings; idealistic; considerate and loving	Neptune in Libra or Pisces Neptune in 2nd or 7th house Venus in Pisces Venus in 12th house
♇ PLUTO	Emotionally intense; may be so scared of being hurt that it's preferable to stay single; can be jealous or suspicious	Pluto in Libra or Scorpio Pluto in 2nd or 7th house Venus in Scorpio Venus in 8th house
ASCENDANT DESCENDANT	Strong emphasis on looking good and being admired; a need for happy, satisfying relationships; charming	Venus in Aries, Leo, Libra or Pisces Venus in 1st, 5th, 7th or 12th house
MC/IC	Can meet partners through work or by being in the public eye; emotions connected to childhood experiences	Venus in Cancer or Capricorn Venus in 4th or 10th house

Use an astrology program to discover which
sign Mars is passing through right now, then refer to the
charts in this section to see how this will affect you.

Your Mars Sign and Your Desires

Mars is the planet of sex and desire.
It also governs motivation, drive and
aggression, so the sign and house of Mars
in your chart, and any aspects it receives
from other planets or angles, describes how
you go about getting what you want in life.
Here, we're looking at how you get
what you want from your partner.

Remember that Mars rules Aries and, traditionally,
Scorpio, so it will operate more strongly when
in one of these two signs.

♂ MARS IN	YOU WANT	HOW YOU GET WHAT YOU WANT	WHAT TURNS YOU ON	CONTROL YOUR
ARIES ♈	Action; things must happen quickly; love of the chase; plenty of exciting and daring sex	By being direct and assertive; being good fun; making the first move	The erogenous zones around your head and ears	Impatience; low boredom threshold; independence; desire for the next sexual conquest
TAURUS ♉	Results; a partner you can rely on; a strong sexual connection; loyalty and stability	Taking control; being patient and playing the waiting game	Having your neck and throat caressed; knowing that you're loved	Possessiveness; urge to be in control; temper, which slowly builds and then explodes
GEMINI ♊	Variety and spontaneity; a lover with a mind of their own, who lets you go your own way sometimes	Winning someone over with the power of words, charm and personality; sexy flirting and banter	Playing with your hands and arms; being with someone who's a match for your own intellect	Desire for no-strings flings when things get boring with your partner
CANCER ♋	Someone you can trust; a happy, stable domestic life; things to always remain the same	By approaching situations and problems from an angle rather than directly; warmth of your personality	Focus on your breasts; sensuous food; being slowly seduced	Nervous energy, moodiness and grumpiness; tendency to react to criticism as if it's a personal attack
LEO ♌	A hot-blooded and responsive partner; sexual games and role-playing; to know that you're number one	Dazzling a partner with everything you can give them; staging tantrums and showdowns	Having your spine stroked; getting your ego massaged; dressing up in glamorous clothes	Urge to be in control at all times; bossiness; sense of superiority
VIRGO ♍	Someone who won't embarrass you, in bed or out; a sexual partner who can stand on their own two feet	By showing yourself in as good a light as possible; dropping hints about what you'd like to happen	Having your stomach stroked; some Mars in Virgo types like to indulge some very kinky tastes	Tendency to nag endlessly instead of lose your temper; irritation; perfectionism

♂ MARS IN	YOU WANT	HOW YOU GET WHAT YOU WANT	WHAT TURNS YOU ON	CONTROL YOUR
LIBRA ♎	To win the love of the person you fancy; a partner who will complement you	By smiling sweetly and agreeing with what others say, then doing your own thing; using your powers of persuasion	Being kissed in the small of your back	Desire to use your charm to manipulate others; urge to start a quarrel whenever things get boring
SCORPIO ♏	To express your emotions with depth and force; a partner who shares your commitment to the relationship	By getting under the skin of the other person; getting angry when things don't go your way	Erotic foreplay; passionate sex; acting out your fantasies	Temper, especially if it's over the top or could cause lasting damage; seething jealousy and resentment
SAGITTARIUS ♐	A fun time in bed with an enthusiastic partner; a lover who matches your intellectual abilities	By making your partner laugh; through your infectious exuberance; being direct and honest	An emphasis on your hips and thighs; rough and tumble foreplay	Tendency to exaggerate in order to get your own way; habit of being too blunt when angry
CAPRICORN ♑	A partner who can take care of themselves; the scope to attain your goals and not be held back	Sheer hard work, determination and absolute focus on your target; never giving up	Older lovers or people in power; someone who is respectable in public and anything but in private	Workaholic tendencies; chilly and dismissive anger
AQUARIUS ♒	To be yourself and not be held back; to express the unconventional areas of your personality	By simply doing your own thing, regardless of the consequences	A partner who is that little bit different; a friend who becomes a lover, or vice versa	Urge to be defiant and to fight battles; uncompromising tendency to distance yourself emotionally
PISCES ♓	An unbreakable emotional and psychic bond with your partner; to be swept away by romance	By being considerate and sensitive; the art of subtle persuasion; appealing to your partner's better nature	Feeling you've been swept off your feet; fantasy or secrecy; the erogenous zones in your feet	Escapist tendencies; reluctance to commit emotionally; promiscuousness

Mars in the Twelve Houses

The house that Mars occupies in your birth chart will show you the area of life in which you focus your emotional drive, as well as how you can assert yourself in sexual and romantic relationships.

EMPHASIS ON
Ambition and career; having an influential partner; being known for your sexuality or affairs

POTENTIAL PITFALLS
Allowing workaholic tendencies to interfere with relationships; demanding that your partner is as successful as you

PLACES TO MEET A PARTNER
At work; during a job interview; while running for election

EMPHASIS ON
Friends, especially those who are dynamic; turning friends into lovers or vice versa

POTENTIAL PITFALLS
Arguments with friends; being bossy or controlling in social settings; competing with a partner's friends

PLACES TO MEET A PARTNER
At a social event, club or society; through a friend

EMPHASIS ON
Sensitivity and a need for privacy; holding back frustrations and anger until they result in a furious outburst

POTENTIAL PITFALLS
Being too withdrawn and shut off emotionally; getting drawn into emotional subterfuge

PLACES TO MEET A PARTNER
While working for a charity or in a charity shop; while helping others

EMPHASIS ON
Getting your own way; getting noticed; making things happen fast

POTENTIAL PITFALLS
Being in too much of a hurry; not appreciating your partner; being accident-prone

PLACES TO MEET A PARTNER
While doing something on your own; while taking a chance

PLACES TO MEET A PARTNER
In a shop while fighting for bargains; at the bank or ATM

EMPHASIS ON
Material values such as making money and owning possessions

POTENTIAL PITFALLS
Boasting about what you own; putting relationships second and acquisitiveness first

PLACES TO MEET A PARTNER
At school; while out on your bike or in your car

EMPHASIS ON
Sticking up for siblings; winning arguments; always being on the go

POTENTIAL PITFALLS
Sarcastic and derisive comments that hurt others' feelings; too many outside interests

10 11 12 1 2 3

Every planet is the natural ruler of one or more houses in the horoscope. For Mars, it's the 1st and 8th houses, so Mars's impact will be boosted if it falls in one of these houses in your chart.

It takes Mars just under two years to complete one circuit of your birth chart, and its energies will be really strong whenever it reaches its natal house or the house opposite.

EMPHASIS ON
Going on adventures; taking risks; pushing the boundaries; a partner from another country or culture

POTENTIAL PITFALLS
Pushing your luck too far; not learning from sexual experience; setting yourself up for disappointment

PLACES TO MEET A PARTNER
In the gym; at a sporting event; at university; on a fly-drive holiday

EMPHASIS ON
Emotional intensity and volatility; a busy and active sex life; passion that can lead to possessiveness

POTENTIAL PITFALLS
Jealousy; sexual frustration that triggers anger; arguments about shared finances

PLACES TO MEET A PARTNER
Somewhere connected with death, taxes or insurance

EMPHASIS ON
Fiery and tempestuous relationships; affairs that start and end quickly

POTENTIAL PITFALLS
Taking out your anger on your partner; rushing into a relationship without thinking it through

PLACES TO MEET A PARTNER
Through your current partner; at an army camp; while sorting out a legal matter

PLACES TO MEET A PARTNER
At work; while working on your car or motorbike; at the doctor's or vet's

EMPHASIS ON
Getting results in whatever you do; competition with colleagues; an excess of nervous energy

POTENTIAL PITFALLS
Eagerness to get ahead leads to cutting corners; burning out; getting angry about your partner's faults

PLACES TO MEET A PARTNER
On the sports field; at a speed-dating session; at a party

EMPHASIS ON
Love and romance; being competitive in love; Impatience with loved ones

POTENTIAL PITFALLS
Confusing love with lust; making emotional commitments in haste and repenting at leisure

PLACES TO MEET A PARTNER
In a DIY store; in an estate agent's

EMPHASIS ON
Channelling your energy into your home and family; wanting a safe domestic environment

POTENTIAL PITFALLS
Going on the defensive at the first sign of trouble; starting a row so you can let off steam

9 8 7 6 5 4

An unaspected planet is just that – it doesn't receive any aspects from other planets or angles. Think of it as being a loner, able to be itself without any outside interference. In the case of Mars, that can mean increased impetus, enthusiasm, haste or anger, depending on the sign and house it's in.

Aspects of Mars – Sexuality

Any angle or planet that is contacted natally by your Mars will be influenced by it, and vice versa. This can emphasize the energy of your Mars or dilute it, depending on the nature of the contact.

INSTANT REMINDER

Conjunction	0°, 8° orb	Energy of the planets is blended
Sextile	60°, 4° orb	Easy-going; opportunities
Square	90°, 8° orb	Tension; trigger for personal growth
Trine	120°, 6° orb	Free-flowing energy
Opposition	180°, 8° orb	Need for balance between opposing forces

MARS ASPECT	INFLUENCE	STRENGTHENED BY
☉ SUN	A need to identify with a cause; a fiery temperament; can be argumentative and impatient; aggressive; emotions can flare	Sun in Aries or Scorpio Sun in 1st or 8th house Mars in Leo Mars in 5th house
☽ MOON	Intrepid, possibly reckless; can be overwhelmed by emotion; defensive under attack; difficult childhood	Moon in Aries or Scorpio Moon in 1st or 8th house Mars in Cancer Mars in 4th house
☿ MERCURY	A lively way of communicating; quick-witted; very direct; can be sarcastic and irritable	Mercury in Aries or Scorpio Mercury in 1st or 8th house Mars in Gemini or Virgo Mars in 3rd or 6th house
♀ VENUS	Sparky; sexy; feisty; enjoys sparring or arguing with a partner and then passionate making up; lively sex life	Venus in Aries or Scorpio Venus in 1st or 8th house Mars in Taurus or Libra Mars in 2nd or 7th house
♃ JUPITER	Good-natured and easy-going; blunt and tactless when defensive; can enjoy sexual adventures or taking sexual risks	Jupiter in Aries or Scorpio Jupiter in 1st or 8th house Mars in Sagittarius Mars in 9th house
♄ SATURN	Relationships can trigger reserve or trepidation; can feel threatened or bullied, or be the one who bullies	Saturn in Aries or Scorpio Saturn in 1st or 8th house Mars in Capricorn Mars in 10th house
♅ URANUS	Daring and unconventional; wants sexual relationships to have an unpredictable or experimental quality	Uranus in Aries or Scorpio Uranus in 1st or 8th house Mars in Aquarius Mars in 11th house
♆ NEPTUNE	Romantic and strongly emotional; can be swept away by love and sex; can want to rescue your partner or be rescued	Neptune in Scorpio Neptune in 8th or 12th house Mars in Pisces Mars in 12th house
♇ PLUTO	Very powerful, intense emotions and sexual drive; determined to conquer problems; temper may be under extreme control or no control at all	Pluto in Scorpio Pluto in 1st or 8th house Mars in Scorpio Mars in 8th house
ASCENDANT DESCENDANT	Energetic; lively; self-centred and subjective; dynamic; relationships may be bad-tempered, volatile or competitive	Mars in Aries or Libra Mars in 1st or 7th house
MC/IC	Hard-working; determined to succeed; goals can crowd out the emotional side of life; problems with parents can interfere with relationships	Mars in Cancer or Capricorn Mars in 4th or 10th house

Uranus and Neptune in the Twelve Houses

These two planets operate in a different way from Venus and Mars. Uranus takes an average of seven years to move through each sign (and eighty-four years to complete a cycle), while Neptune's pace is even slower, taking around fourteen years to go through each sign (and 164.8 years to complete a cycle). Therefore, the meanings of their signs are too general for this book, and we're going to focus instead on Uranus and Neptune in the houses, and when making aspects to other planets.

✦

Uranus and Neptune are complete opposites. Uranus in a house shows the area of life in which you want to be an individual; your own person. Neptune shows where you want to merge with others and show sensitivity.

✦

URANUS IN THE TWELVE HOUSES

May meet a partner in unexpected ways while travelling; partner may practise an unconventional religion or way of life

Can dislike taking responsibility for others; a need to be independent and a resistance to being told what to do

An attraction to unusual sexual relationships or maybe no sex at all; can be drawn to partners who represent a sexual taboo

Partners must be friends too, and hold their own intellectually; you may avoid emotional relationships and focus on friendships

You're drawn to unusual or even outrageous partners; relationships have an erratic quality with sudden stops/starts

An interest in unusual partners or emotional situations; secrets can play a big role in your emotional life; your public persona may be very different from your private life

Moodiness and a strong need to follow your own path rather than anyone else's; relationships with colleagues can be up and down

A sense of being an outsider or different from others; independent and can be eccentric; you tend to stand out from the crowd

Can have an on-off approach to love or blow hot and cold emotionally; attracted to lovers who are controversial or surprising

A strong determination to honour your values, even if others don't agree; can be stubborn and obstinate; erratic emotions

Very original and interesting personality; a deep need for emotional freedom and hatred of being tied down

A dislike of too much emotional commitment; you like to ruffle feathers deliberately when things get boring; you may live apart from your partner

10 11 12 1 2 3 4 5 6 7 8 9

NEPTUNE IN THE TWELVE HOUSES

Idealistic; a long journey can lead to a significant relationship; your partner may be connected with education, travel or politics

May be attracted to partners who are well known; mixed feelings about a parent can affect sexual relationships

Can seek sexual relationships that are ethereal or otherworldly; emphasis on seduction

Friends turn into romantic partners; a need to rescue the world can lead to immense kindness or fractured relationships

A yearning to immerse yourself in your partner or to rescue them; your partner may have a religious or spiritual belief, or seek escapism in other ways

Boundaries between you and partners can be weak, so you don't know where you end and they begin; easily influenced; compassionate; kind; idealistic

Difficulties in handling day-to-day problems; marked difference in status between you and your partner

Sensitive and romantic; easily hurt but can also be unaware of causing pain; can have an elusive quality that makes you hard to know

Idealistic and highly romantic; unrealistic expectations lead to disappointment; you pretend relationship problems don't exist

Relationships can be tied up with money, especially if you are the provider; fluctuating feelings about what and who is important

Highly sensitive; easily hurt but may try to gloss over it; impressionable and can be gullible

Confusion and inaccuracies cause communication problems; dislike of saying the wrong thing or upsetting others

12 11 10 9 8 7 6 5 4 3 2 1

Aspects of Uranus – Independently Yours

If Uranus forms an aspect to a planet or angle in your chart, it adds an extra spark to the way you connect with loved ones, but also how you strive to be separate, to stand out from the crowd and to be independent and detached. Aspects from Uranus to Neptune and Pluto aren't listed here because they affect whole generations and don't have a personal influence on us.

✦

Use the descriptions on the following pages not only when analyzing your own or your partner's chart, but also when interpreting transits to your chart from Uranus to see how they will affect you emotionally.

✦

URANUS ASPECT	INFLUENCE	STRENGTHENED BY
☉ SUN	A drive to be yourself, even if that causes problems with others; a need for independence	Sun in Aquarius Sun in 11th house Uranus in Leo Uranus in 5th house
☽ MOON	Up and down emotionally; moody and cantankerous; dislike of too much togetherness; may prefer to live alone	Moon in Aquarius Moon in 11th house Uranus in Cancer Uranus in 4th house
☿ MERCURY	A quirky way of doing things; hates being told what to do; a need for your own space and for time to think	Mercury in Aquarius Mercury in 11th house Uranus in Gemini or Virgo Uranus in 3rd or 6th house
♀ VENUS	You need a partner who is charming and charismatic, and understands your yearning for independence; your changeable emotions can upset partners	Venus in Aquarius Venus in 11th house Uranus in Taurus or Libra Uranus in 2nd or 7th house
♂ MARS	Daring and unconventional; you want sexual relationships to have an unpredictable or experimental quality	Uranus in Aries or Scorpio Uranus in 1st or 8th house Mars in Aquarius Mars in 11th house
♃ JUPITER	Huge drive for independence and to be unfettered by convention; sparky; clever; outspoken; wilful	Uranus in Sagittarius Uranus in 9th house Jupiter in Aquarius Jupiter in 11th house
♄ SATURN	Tension between being conventional and breaking the rules; can be emotionally detached, preferring logic to love	Uranus in Capricorn Uranus in 10th house Saturn in Capricorn or Aquarius Saturn in 10th or 11th house
ASCENDANT DESCENDANT	Magnetic personality; bright; unusual; relationships can be erratic, or start/end without warning; may prefer to be single	Uranus in Aries or Libra Uranus in 1st or 7th house
MC/IC	A disruptive or unconventional childhood can lead to a desire to live alone or difficulty settling down; you need space to breathe and be yourself	Uranus in Cancer or Capricorn Uranus in 4th or 10th house

Aspects of Neptune –
Your Urge to Merge

The energy of Neptune is around refining, merging and becoming at one with another person, so when Neptune makes contact with a planet or angle in your chart, it describes how you tune into someone. Aspects from Neptune to Uranus and Pluto aren't listed here because they affect entire generations and don't have a personal influence on us.

✦

Neptune can have a nebulous, spaced-out influence. It can also show where we trip ourselves up by being defeatist or sabotaging our own efforts. Square and opposition aspects, in particular, can indicate where we let others undermine us.

✦

NEPTUNE ASPECT	INFLUENCE	STRENGTHENED BY
☉ SUN	Kind and compassionate; can be highly emotional and overly affected by others; partner may struggle with addiction	Sun in Pisces Sun in 12th house Neptune in 5th or 12th house
☽ MOON	Highly emotional and sensitive; can struggle to deal with harsh realities; may want to rescue others or be rescued	Moon in Pisces Moon in 12th house Neptune in 4th or 12th house
☿ MERCURY	Imaginative and intuitive; facts can be distorted or manipulated, leading to confusion or mistrust; there can be a reluctance to say anything hurtful	Mercury in Pisces Mercury in 12th house Neptune in 3rd or 12th house
♀ VENUS	Emotionally sensitive, with a yearning for happy endings; love of romance; idealistic; considerate and loving	Venus in Pisces Venus in 12th house Neptune in Libra or Pisces Neptune in 2nd, 7th or 12th house
♂ MARS	Romantic and strongly emotional; swept away by love and sex, and overly influenced by your partner; may want to rescue others or be rescued	Mars in Pisces Mars in 12th house Neptune in Scorpio Neptune in 1st, 8th or 12th house
♃ JUPITER	Idealistic, optimistic and prone to exaggeration; can be drawn to partners who have mystical or spiritual beliefs	Jupiter in Pisces Jupiter in 12th house Neptune in Sagittarius Neptune in 9th or 12th house
♄ SATURN	An ability to combine practicality and inspiration; there can be emotional tension; disappointments can hit hard	Saturn in Pisces Saturn in 12th house Neptune in Capricorn Neptune in 10th or 12th house
ASCENDANT DESCENDANT	Your elusive quality means partners struggle to fully know you; tendency to be all things to all people; idealistic	Neptune in Libra Neptune in 1st, 7th or 12th house
MC/IC	Possibly extreme sensitivity about the past; yearning for an idealized home life; loving and affectionate	Neptune in Capricorn Neptune in 4th, 10th or 12th house

The Descendant

Often people are interested in knowing about their Ascendant, which describes the face they show to the world, but don't know anything about their Descendant. Yet it's the Descendant that has such an impact in relationships because it describes what we're looking for and how we behave with partners. Look for your Descendant in the list opposite to learn about your particular style of relationship.

Remember that the sign on the Descendant is opposite to the one on the Ascendant, so they balance each other.

HERE ARE THE PAIRINGS:

Aries	Libra	Taurus	Scorpio	Gemini	Sagittarius
Cancer	Capricorn	Leo	Aquarius	Virgo	Pisces

SIGN	ON DESCENDANT	STRENGTHENED BY
ARIES ♈	You are assertive, outgoing and can be self-centred	Mars in Aries Mars in 1st, 5th or 7th house
TAURUS ♉	You need emotional stability and a partner you can utterly rely on	Sun and/or Venus in Taurus Venus in 2nd, 5th or 7th house
GEMINI ♊	You need a clever and witty partner who won't crowd you emotionally	Mercury in Gemini Mercury in 3rd, 5th or 7th house
CANCER ♋	Love and security are your main aims, as well as feeling protected and cared for	Moon in Cancer Moon in 4th, 5th or 7th house
LEO ♌	Your partner must love, appreciate and admire you, and vice versa	Sun and/or Venus in Leo Sun in 5th or 7th house
VIRGO ♍	You're very selective about who you hook up with, but can also be critical of them	Mercury in Virgo Mercury and/or Venus in 5th or 7th house
LIBRA ♎	Your partner must be easy on the eye and polite, and not want to possess you	Sun and/or Venus in Libra Venus in 7th house
SCORPIO ♏	You need intensity, drama and loyalty, and a deep emotional connection	Pluto in Scorpio Pluto in 7th or 8th house
SAGITTARIUS ♐	You're attracted by a partner from another country or someone who is great company	Jupiter in Sagittarius Jupiter in 7th house
CAPRICORN ♑	Your partner must be respectable, sensible, successful and not overly emotional	Saturn in Libra or Capricorn Saturn in 5th or 7th house
AQUARIUS ♒	Partnerships can be tricky because of your need for independence and emotional space	Uranus in Libra or Aquarius Uranus in 5th or 7th house
PISCES ♓	Relationships can be muddled or messy; you need a partner who is compassionate and patient	Neptune in Pisces Neptune in 5th, 7th or 12th house

3

Work and career

For many of us, it's essential to earn a living. But there's a world of difference between doing a job because we have to and doing it because we love it. If you want to make your working life more fulfilling, not only by finding a job that suits you down to the ground but also by improving your relationship with your colleagues and boss, you will need to know where to look on your horoscope.

Astrology and Work

What is hard work and an unrelenting slog for one person can be an absolute joy for another. It all depends on where our abilities lie and what we enjoy doing for a living, and the answers to those questions lie in our horoscope.

As you will discover in this chapter, three planets have a particular role to play in our attitude to our work and career:

* The Sun – how and where we want to shine
* Mercury – how we think and communicate with others
* Saturn – our sense of responsibility and work ethic

We will also be looking at the angle of the birth chart known as the MC, because this describes our ambitions and how we want to be regarded by others. Your own MC is like a flag waving at the top of your birth chart, announcing who you are and what you can offer to the world. And you're about to discover what that flag is proclaiming!

Before we move on to the rest of this chapter, here's a list of the types of job that are best suited to each sign. Don't be confused if your Sun, Mercury, Saturn and MC are all in different signs. Each one offers you scope and suggests different ways for you to make the most of your chart at work.

If you have to do a job to pay the bills rather than because it's something you love, expressing your Sun sign in your spare time will give you a fulfilling vocation.

ARIES
Entrepreneur; innovator; selling cars; car mechanic; surgeon; welder; fire service; running your own business; athlete; the army

TAURUS
Horticulture; agriculture; farming; floristry; fashion designer; working with textiles; singing; massage; finance; aromatherapy

GEMINI
Teacher; writer; journalist; blogger; broadcaster; linguist; taxi driver; postal service; interpreter

CANCER
Nurse; nanny; teacher of small children; foster parent; cook; interior designer; estate agent; genealogist; historian

LEO
Actor; theatre production or direction; dancer; painter; professional athlete or sports person; orchestral conductor; teacher; cardiologist

VIRGO
Personal assistant; statistician; accountant; nurse; laboratory technician; dietician; pharmacist; vet; clinician; biologist; dental hygienist

LIBRA
Judge; lawyer; barrister; solicitor; mediator; negotiator; jeweller; fashion designer; model; artist; social worker; couples counsellor; HR

SCORPIO
Psychologist; psychiatrist; forensic pathologist; funeral director; spy; detective; police; archaeologist; financial adviser; banking; tax official

SAGITTARIUS
Travel agent or rep; pilot; teacher; university lecturer; librarian; bookseller; writer; publisher; racehorse trainer; jockey; bookie; lawyer

CAPRICORN
Politician; civil servant; scientist; osteopath; chiropractor; dentist; dermatologist; architect; surveyor; builder; town planner

AQUARIUS
Environmentalist; humanitarian; activist; campaigner; technician; scientist; astrologer; astro-physicist; television presenter; television producer; IT; robotics

PISCES
Charity worker; monk, nun or priest; perfumier; dancer; actor; painter; photographer; swimmer; the navy; fishing; reflexologist; podiatrist; social worker; counsellor

Your Sun Sign and How You Want to Shine

You might know this as your star sign, rather than your Sun sign. But whatever you want to call it, this sign describes your life path. It represents your essential self, so even if you don't pay attention to anything else in your chart, you need to concentrate on your Sun sign. It describes so many essential elements of your personality, and if you don't express this sign fully you will always feel that something important is missing. Among other things, your Sun sign describes your goals, your need to express yourself, and the areas of life in which you want to shine. And that, of course, includes your work and career.

✦

As the transiting Sun returns to your own sign each year, all the career themes of your sign will be activated, offering you the chance to express them in fresh, new ways.

✦

SUN IN	YOUR EGO NEEDS	CONTROL YOUR
ARIES ♈	Attention; recognition; to get things done in the way you want; independence	Impatience; need to be right; desire to always beat the competition; reluctance to learn from mistakes
TAURUS ♉	Stability; to see the results of your efforts; to honour your values; achievement and self-respect	Resistance to change; tendency to stick to what you know and trust
GEMINI ♊	Versatility and room to breathe; to share your ideas; to communicate your thoughts	Flightiness; tendency to be distracted; desire to avoid difficult decisions
CANCER ♋	To be able to nurture others in your own way; to feel that you belong and are in familiar territory	Defensiveness; moodiness; tendency to worry about everything
LEO ♌	To be admired and for your efforts to be appreciated and applauded; creative expression and satisfaction	Ego and need to be in the spotlight; bossiness; obstinacy; pride; desire to do everything yourself and not delegate
VIRGO ♍	To know that you're doing your very best; to help others; quiet appreciation from co-workers	Tendency to find fault, not only with yourself but with colleagues; worrying about tiny details

SUN IN	YOUR EGO NEEDS	CONTROL YOUR
LIBRA ♎	A reputation for being courteous and pleasant; to feel that you handle people well; to get results in your own way	Indecision, caused by your ability to see both sides of any question; desire to be liked
SCORPIO ♏	To be in control of yourself and others; to feel that you're an essential cog in a big wheel; some form of transformation	Emotional demands; professional jealousy; desire to manipulative others; willpower; suspicions
SAGITTARIUS ♐	To be independent and true to yourself; credit for your knowledge; to be versatile; to express your innate optimism; challenges	Belief that you always know best; tendency to put your foot in your mouth; candour; tendency to ignore inconvenient details
CAPRICORN ♑	The respect you deserve; a reputation for being a hard worker; the chance to do things your way; to achieve your ambitions	Conviction that you aren't good enough; tendency to put yourself down; shyness; pessimism; fear of rejection; need to always do things the tried and trusted way
AQUARIUS ♒	To be a free spirit; to do things your way; to break new ground; to be respected for your intelligence and innovation	Determination to always be in the right; tendency to assume that others are stupid; dogmatism; independence; contrariness
PISCES ♓	To use your intuition; to show your sensitivity; to let things flow rather than plan them rigidly in advance; to be taken seriously	Desire to escape from unpleasant realities; vagueness; scattiness; gullibility; defeatism; tendency to be overwhelmed emotionally during a crisis

The Sun in the Twelve Houses

Look up the position of your Sun in terms
of the house it occupies in your chart
to discover how this influences
your goals and behaviour
at work.

EMPHASIS ON
Keen to prove yourself
through hard work; reliable;
responsible; stable; working
for a big company or brand

EMPHASIS ON
Working as part of a group;
a need to be with kindred
spirits; far-reaching plans;
kind to colleagues;
humanitarian ideals

**POTENTIAL
PITFALLS**
Workaholic
tendencies;
your career takes
over your life;
reluctance to
delegate

**POTENTIAL
PITFALLS**
Individuality turns into
eccentricity; bossy;
intellectually superior;
too progressive

EMPHASIS ON
Being able to work
alone; keeping other
people's confidences;
work as a healer or
therapist

POTENTIAL PITFALLS
Being manipulated by others;
reluctance to publicize your
talents; inability to deal
with unpleasant situations

POTENTIAL PITFALLS
Only seeing situations from
your own viewpoint;
in too much of a hurry to
get things done

EMPHASIS ON
Making an impact; taking
the lead; innovation
and enterprise; being
an entrepreneur; self-
employment

**POTENTIAL
PITFALLS**
Single-mindedness turns
to stubbornness; judging
yourself and others by
material values

**POTENTIAL
PITFALLS**
Lack of
concentration;
tendency to chat; a
need to have fingers
in too many pies

EMPHASIS ON
Being true to your beliefs;
receiving fair payment;
work in banking and
finance, or in luxury items

EMPHASIS ON
Communicating with the
people around you; a need to be
flexible at work; work in the media
or sales; working with your hands

10
11
12
1
2
3

✦

If your Sun falls at the very end of a house, the interpretation for the Sun in the following house may ring more true for you. The size of the houses can vary from one system to the next so you need to make allowances for this.

✦

EMPHASIS ON
A career that broadens your knowledge; working with people from other cultures; enthusiasm and optimism; travel; further education

POTENTIAL PITFALLS
Unrealistic idealism leading to disappointment; struggling to meet ambitious goals

EMPHASIS ON
Work that feels significant; a sense of accomplishment; sharing resources with business partners; work in banking or insurance

POTENTIAL PITFALLS
Emotional intensity that creates dramas; not knowing how to relinquish control

EMPHASIS ON
Blossoming around others; creating harmony and a peaceful atmosphere; cooperation; business partnerships; HR

POTENTIAL PITFALLS
Being too conciliatory; relying on colleagues emotionally; giving away your power to others

POTENTIAL PITFALLS
Living for your work; identifying too much with your job; wanting praise

EMPHASIS ON
Flourishing in a work environment; putting everything into your job; being of service; work in medicine

POTENTIAL PITFALLS
Letting your ego get out of hand; making things all about you; frustration if your talents are overlooked

POTENTIAL PITFALLS
Not wanting to leave a job even when it would suit your career; not wanting to change old working systems; pulling rank

EMPHASIS ON
Being noticed and respected; standing out from the crowd; creativity; jobs connected with the arts

EMPHASIS ON
Wanting to feel that you belong; taking care of your workmates; a career connected with homes and families

9 8 7 6 5 4

Aspects of the Sun – Your Work

Any aspects that the Sun makes to
another planet or one of the angles in
your chart will give you a valuable
insight into your sense of identity and
the way you operate at work.

Always consider the nature of the Sun in a chart before analyzing
the aspects it makes, so you can see how it will react to the planets
it aspects. As an example, a confident and self-reliant Sun (such as
in Aries or Leo) is less likely to be hampered by a difficult aspect
than a shy and uncertain Sun (such as in Capricorn or Pisces).

SUN ASPECT	INFLUENCE	STRENGTHENED BY
☽ MOON	Creative; energetic; very focused; emotionally charged; work can involve children, families or homes	Sun in Cancer Sun in 4th house Moon in Leo Moon in 5th house
☿ MERCURY	A born communicator; can talk too much; needs to keep on the move; great at selling and negotiating	Sun in Gemini or Virgo Sun in 3rd or 6th house Mercury in Leo Mercury in 5th house
♀ VENUS	Courteous; considerate; good-hearted; work can involve fashion, luxury, the creative arts or music	Sun in Taurus or Libra Sun in 2nd or 7th house Venus in Leo Venus in 5th house
♂ MARS	Industrious; full of energy which needs positive direction; aggressive; strong-willed; a risk-taker	Sun in Aries or Scorpio Sun in 1st or 8th house Mars in Leo Mars in 1st or 5th house
♃ JUPITER	Confident; self-assured; optimistic; can be pompous or arrogant; work involving travel, horses or publishing	Sun in Sagittarius Sun in 9th house Jupiter in Leo Jupiter in 5th or 9th house
♄ SATURN	Hard-working; responsible; can take on too much; can lack confidence; self-expression can be blocked	Sun in Capricorn Sun in 10th house Saturn in Leo Saturn in 5th or 10th house
♅ URANUS	Independent; self-motivated; not good at being told what to do; self-employment	Sun in Aquarius Sun in 11th house Uranus in Leo Uranus in 5th house
♆ NEPTUNE	Impressionable; highly creative; sensitive; charity work; religious or spiritual vocation; photography	Sun in Pisces Sun in 12th house Neptune in 5th or 12th house
♇ PLUTO	Intense and driven; a need to wield power and control; tax, psychotherapy or taboo topics	Sun in Scorpio Sun in 8th house Pluto in Leo Pluto in 5th or 8th house
ASCENDANT DESCENDANT	A need to connect with others; best suited to working as part of a team; work involving fashion	Sun in Libra Sun in 7th house
MC/IC	A great desire to be seen and to do your best; ambitious; drawn to the spotlight; managerial work	Sun in Capricorn Sun in 10th house

Your Mercury Sign at Work

Mercury is the planet of communication, so its position in your birth chart has a lot to say about the way you think and connect with other people. Mercury plays an important role at work because if you can't talk to a colleague or client, how can you communicate with them?

✦

Consider the element that your Mercury belongs to, as well as its sign, so you can see if it communicates enthusiastically (fire), in a grounded fashion (earth), in an intellectual way (air) or emotionally (water).

✦

SIGN	YOUR WORKING TALENTS	POSSIBLE PITFALLS
ARIES ♈	Fast thinking and talking; you want quick responses from colleagues; good at coming up with new ideas	Can be too quick to act and too impatient to listen; great at starting new projects but can soon lose interest
TAURUS ♉	Steady and logical thinking; you need time to process new ideas; happiest with people you know well	Can be too conservative; reluctance to try anything new, such as new working systems
GEMINI ♊	A born communicator; you love bouncing ideas off colleagues; great at networking; versatile	Good at starting projects but bad at finishing them; too chatty; easily distracted and bored
CANCER ♋	Kind and sympathetic to colleagues; excellent at keeping records; interested in cooking and the home	Emotions can get the better of you, making you moody or tearful; can be subjective and emotionally biased
LEO ♌	A flair for the dramatic and creative; organizational skills; good at encouraging workmates and clients	Can think that you know best; a need to be in charge; a belief in your own publicity
VIRGO ♍	An eye for detail and a meticulous approach; objective and practical ideas; reliable	Too much analysis and not enough action; can be a perfectionist; critical of colleagues
LIBRA ♎	Able to see all points of view; good at liaising with others; courteous; diplomatic and tactful	Indecisive; vacillation because you don't want to cause offence; can depend too much on others
SCORPIO ♏	Penetrating mind; great powers of concentration and focus; verbal vehemence and passion	Can develop tunnel vision; can be reluctant to change your mind; can be sarcastic and cutting
SAGITTARIUS ♐	An inquisitive mind; love of learning new things; open-minded; positive and confident; versatile	Your love of the truth can make you blunt; idealistic; reluctant to tackle tedious details or deliver bad news
CAPRICORN ♑	Acute and sharp mind; a serious outlook; excellent at business dealings; careful; ambitious ideas	Delays or setbacks can lead to pessimism; can get bogged down in doing things properly
AQUARIUS ♒	Far-seeing, innovative; interested in technology and new systems; ability to see through hypocrisy	Your radical and progressive ideas can frighten others; mentally obstinate
PISCES ♓	Considerate and helpful to colleagues; an interest in others' welfare; great empathy and intuition	You believe what you want to believe; forgetful and disorganized; your imagination can run away with you

Mercury in the Twelve Houses

Whichever house Mercury occupies
in your chart will reveal the area
of life that interests you,
where you have a natural
talent, and which therefore
might be a good working
environment.

WHERE YOUR SKILLS LIE
Business negotiations; using
your brain; civil service;
public speaking; trade deals

**WHERE YOUR
SKILLS LIE**
Humanitarian work;
technology; computers;
politics; organizing
or running groups

EMPHASIZED BY
Sun and/or Mercury
in Capricorn
Sun in 10th house
Saturn in Gemini

EMPHASIZED BY
Sun and/or Mercury
in Aquarius
Sun in 11th house
Uranus in 11th house

**WHERE YOUR
SKILLS LIE**
Charity work; prison
visitor; hospice worker;
spiritual advisor or leader;
intellectual research

EMPHASIZED BY
Sun and/or Mercury
in Pisces
Sun in 12th house
Neptune in 12th house

EMPHASIZED BY
Sun and/or Mercury in Aries
Mars in Gemini
Sun in 1st house

**WHERE YOUR
SKILLS LIE**
Being active and
engaged in everything;
self-promotion;
self-employment

EMPHASIZED BY
Sun and/or Mercury
in Taurus
Venus in Taurus
Sun and/or Venus
in 2nd house

EMPHASIZED BY
Sun and/or
Mercury in Gemini
Sun in 3rd house

**WHERE YOUR
SKILLS LIE**
Finance; sales, especially
on the phone; luxury goods;
land agent; estate agent;
throat specialist; singer

WHERE YOUR SKILLS LIE
Primary education; journalism;
newsreader; public transport;
working with languages

These are suggestions to trigger your imagination. To come up with more ideas, simply combine the meanings of Mercury with the house it occupies in your chart.

WHERE YOUR SKILLS LIE
Higher education; travel guide; travel agent; philosophy; publishing; life coach; international trade

WHERE YOUR SKILLS LIE
Establishing deep emotional links with others; psychotherapy; phone helpline; finance

EMPHASIZED BY
Sun and/or Mercury in Sagittarius
Sun in 9th house
Jupiter in 9th house

EMPHASIZED BY
Sun and/or Mercury in Scorpio
Sun in 8th house
Pluto in 8th house

WHERE YOUR SKILLS LIE
Advocacy; the legal profession; relationship counselling; the diplomatic service

EMPHASIZED BY
Sun and/or Mercury in Libra
Sun and/or Venus in 7th house

EMPHASIZED BY
Sun and/or Mercury in Virgo
Sun in 6th house

WHERE YOUR SKILLS LIE
Non-fiction writer; health-related topics; secretarial work; talking to colleagues and clients

EMPHASIZED BY
Sun and/or Mercury in Leo
Sun in 5th house

EMPHASIZED BY
Sun and/or Mercury in Cancer
Sun in 4th house
Moon in Gemini

WHERE YOUR SKILLS LIE
Teaching or looking after children; writer; romantic novelist; professional gambler

WHERE YOUR SKILLS LIE
Estate agent; dealer in mobile homes; any job connected with home or family; working from home

Aspects of Mercury – Your Career

Any natal planet or angle aspected by Mercury will be coloured by it. This table shows how these aspects will affect your ability to communicate with others.

✦

Learn to deepen these interpretations by considering the signs of both Mercury and the other planet or angle, so you can understand the dynamics of that particular combination.

✦

MERCURY ASPECT	INFLUENCE	STRENGTHENED BY
☉ **SUN**	A born communicator; can talk too much; a need to keep on the move; great at selling and negotiating	Mercury in Leo Mercury in 5th house Sun in Gemini or Virgo Sun in 3rd or 6th house
☽ **MOON**	Great intellectual ability; intuitive; astute; good at discussing emotions; drawn to home-related careers	Mercury in Cancer Mercury in 4th house Moon in Gemini or Virgo Moon in 3rd or 6th house
♀ **VENUS**	Good at putting others at their ease; excellent for fashion, styling or hairdressing; charming	Mercury in Taurus or Libra Mercury in 2nd or 7th house Venus in Gemini or Virgo
♂ **MARS**	Direct way of talking; good at debates and arguments; confident; manual dexterity; jobs involving transport	Mercury in Aries Mercury in 1st house Mars in Gemini Mars in 3rd house
♃ **JUPITER**	Big ideas; clever; active mind; people skills; optimistic; lecturing; writing; publicity	Mercury in Sagittarius Mercury in 9th house Jupiter in Gemini Jupiter in 3rd or 9th house
♄ **SATURN**	Common sense; straight talking; precise; can be prone to worry; expertise with words or speech	Mercury in Capricorn Mercury in 10th house Saturn in Gemini Saturn in 3rd house
♅ **URANUS**	Intellectual ability; you have mental scope and vision; can be erratic; gift for technology and gadgets	Mercury in Aquarius Mercury in 11th house Uranus in Gemini Uranus in 3rd house
♆ **NEPTUNE**	Imaginative; intuitive; creative; open to new ideas; lines of truth can be blurred; writer; psychic	Mercury in Pisces Mercury in 12th house Neptune in 3rd or 12th house
♇ **PLUTO**	Perceptive; sharp thinker; questioning; good powers of concentration; crime writer; researcher	Mercury in Scorpio Mercury in 8th house Pluto in 3rd house
ASCENDANT DESCENDANT	Chatty; lively; restless; good at connecting with others; talking therapies; health matters; negotiator	Mercury in Virgo or Libra Mercury in 1st or 6th house
MC/IC	Nervous energy; good communicator; estate agent; spokesperson; work with families or the past	Mercury in Cancer or Capricorn Mercury in 4th or 10th house

Your Saturn Sign and Your Career

Here's a heavyweight planet! Saturn
gives us resilience, a sense of responsibility
and backbone so we can face up to problems.
Although Saturn can bring delays and
disappointments, it teaches us to learn
from experience and, metaphorically,
to stand on our own two feet. All of which
are important when we're at work.

As well as reading about your natal Saturn, you can
also refer to this table when you want to know how
your work will be affected by transiting Saturn.

SIGN	YOUR WORKING TALENTS	POSSIBLE PITFALLS
ARIES ♈	Ambitious and competitive; you want to get ahead and will stick at it until you do; self-reliant	A stop-go quality; easily discouraged by setbacks; not happy when given orders or guidance
TAURUS ♉	You like to take things slowly and play safe; practical and sensible; you dislike letting others down	Resistant to change; dogged and industrious; work can take precedence so you forget to have fun
GEMINI ♊	Clear thinking; intellectual; clever with words; good for teaching and writing; speech therapist	Reluctance to say what you really think or commit yourself; can doubt your mental and verbal abilities
CANCER ♋	Tenacious and persistent in achieving a goal; cautious about taking risks; work with families	Your need for security can clash with your desire for success; home life can play second fiddle to work
LEO ♌	Organized and practical; your pride won't let you slip up; strong-willed; good at taking charge of others	A fear of authority figures; chilly emotionally; can be autocratic; you can take life too seriously
VIRGO ♍	A hard worker; careful and conscientious; methodical; painstaking; an interest in health matters	Can be a workaholic; can pay too much attention to small details; fear of not being good enough
LIBRA ♎	Keen to play fair by others; good judge of character; courteous and kind; good at mediation and legal work	It can be hard to assert your authority; working partnerships can cause problems; indecisive
SCORPIO ♏	Controlled and reserved emotionally; professional persona; interest in medicine or insurance	You don't make it easy for others to know you; can be pessimistic; wary of letting others take control
SAGITTARIUS ♐	Honest, philosophical and straightforward; strong intellectual powers; writing; teaching; academic research	Moralistic and self-righteous; fear of trusting others to do the right thing; can be cynical and sceptical
CAPRICORN ♑	Disciplined; conscientious; reliable; responsible; organized; a need to do things by the book	Hard to switch off from work; fear of not deserving your good reputation; can have inflexible opinions
AQUARIUS ♒	You want to do things properly but in your own way; original; independent; interested in technology	You want to be true to yourself yet don't want to be alienated from others; can be obstinate
PISCES ♓	Intuitive; strong empathy; good at turning ideas into reality; creative; social worker; counsellor	Not good at facing facts; weak boundaries with others; can be defeatist in the face of problems

Saturn in the Twelve Houses

The house position of Saturn in your chart shows where your sense of responsibility lies, and therefore where you can excel at work.

AREAS OF RESPONSIBILITY
Big business; bureaucracy; civil service; government; architecture; the elderly; can be too responsible

AREAS OF RESPONSIBILITY
Looking after a group or society; science; technology; computers; work involving friends; social life can suffer

EMPHASIZED BY
Saturn in Capricorn
Sun in Capricorn
Sun in 10th house

EMPHASIZED BY
Saturn in Aquarius
Uranus in Aquarius
Uranus in 10th house

AREAS OF RESPONSIBILITY
Working alone or behind the scenes; hospice, hospital or prison work; can be too serious and anxious

EMPHASIZED BY
Saturn in Pisces
Neptune in 10th house

EMPHASIZED BY
Saturn in Aries
or Capricorn
Mars in 10th house

AREAS OF RESPONSIBILITY
Personal responsibility; disciplined; can work too hard or too long, or feel you aren't good enough

EMPHASIZED BY
Saturn in Taurus
Venus in 10th house

Saturn tends to err on the side of caution and can also show what we fear, so its house position can reveal where we tend to do too much or the areas of life that can make us anxious, even when work isn't involved.

AREAS OF RESPONSIBILITY
Financially responsible; good at handling budgets; can be miserly or grudging; resistant to change

EMPHASIZED BY
Saturn in Gemini
Mercury in Capricorn
Mercury in 10th house

AREAS OF RESPONSIBILITY
Excellent at networking, PR and marketing; local transport; can worry about being misunderstood

As Saturn transits each house in your chart, the relevant working areas are highlighted. Refer to this table to see how Saturn might be affecting your working life at the moment.

AREAS OF RESPONSIBILITY
Philosophy; the law; higher education; long-distance travel; publishing; can have mental exhaustion

EMPHASIZED BY
Saturn in Sagittarius
Jupiter in Capricorn
Jupiter in 10th house

AREAS OF RESPONSIBILITY
Other people's money, e.g. mortgages, bank accounts and wills; funeral director; can fear emotional intensity

EMPHASIZED BY
Saturn in Scorpio
Pluto in 10th house

AREAS OF RESPONSIBILITY
Legal work; negotiations; counselling; working with men; personal relationships can suffer because of work

EMPHASIZED BY
Saturn in Libra
Venus in Capricorn
Venus in 10th house

EMPHASIZED BY
Saturn in Virgo
Mercury in Capricorn
Mercury in 10th house

AREAS OF RESPONSIBILITY
Taking care of details; health visitor; medicine or pharmacy; vet; can sacrifice personal life for work

EMPHASIZED BY
Saturn in Leo
Sun in Capricorn
Sun in 10th house

EMPHASIZED BY
Saturn in Cancer
Moon in Capricorn
Moon in 10th house

AREAS OF RESPONSIBILITY
Precise creative work; artistic or theatre director; looking after children; not having enough fun in life

AREAS OF RESPONSIBILITY
Work dealing with families, homelessness, housing, women; can become too emotionally detached

9 8 7 6 5 4

Aspects of Saturn — Your Career

Aspects to your natal Saturn from other
planets or from the angles reveal how
your Saturn is shaped by these influences.
In turn, Saturn will affect the planets or angles
it contacts. Remember, here we're looking
at how your Saturn aspects affect
your working life.

SATURN ASPECT	INFLUENCE	STRENGTHENED BY
☉ **SUN**	Hard-working; responsible; can take on too much; can lack confidence; self-expression can be blocked	Sun in Capricorn Sun in 10th house Saturn in Leo or Capricorn Saturn in 5th or 10th house
☽ **MOON**	Industrious; perfectionist; can have a need to work and do well; can be distant or formal with colleagues	Moon in Capricorn Moon in 10th house Saturn in Cancer Saturn in 4th or 10th house
☿ **MERCURY**	Common sense; straight talking; precise; can be prone to worry; expertise with words or speech	Mercury in Capricorn Mercury in 10th house Saturn in Gemini Saturn in 3rd house
♀ **VENUS**	Great for careful creative work; you may doubt your talents; emotional restraint with colleagues and clients	Venus in Capricorn Venus in 10th house Saturn in Taurus or Libra Saturn in 2nd or 7th house
♂ **MARS**	Powerful drive to do well; can face frustration and delays; career can have peaks and troughs	Mars in Capricorn Mars in 10th house Saturn in Aries Saturn in 1st house
♃ **JUPITER**	Driven and motivated; capable of great things; can be a clash between optimism and pessimism	Jupiter in Capricorn Jupiter in 10th house Saturn in Sagittarius Saturn in 9th house
♅ **URANUS**	Determined and ambitious; your energy and approach can be erratic; excellent for technology and science	Uranus in Capricorn Uranus in 10th house Saturn in Aquarius Saturn in 11th house
♆ **NEPTUNE**	Can turn inspiration into concrete results; emotional tension and reticence; gifts for music and mathematics	Neptune in Capricorn Neptune in 10th house Saturn in Pisces Saturn in 12th house
♇ **PLUTO**	Responsible and careful; strong sense of responsibility can cause frustration; strong-willed	Pluto in 10th house Saturn in Scorpio Saturn in 8th house
ASCENDANT DESCENDANT	Practical; organized; methodical; can be reticent when dealing with others; restrained emotions	Saturn in Aries or Libra Saturn in 1st or 7th house
MC/IC	Industrious; efficient; disciplined; highly ambitious, but your private life can suffer as a result	Saturn in Cancer or Capricorn Saturn in 4th or 10th house

The MC

If you want to understand what you're aiming for in life, and how you make the most of your working potential, you need to pay special attention to the angle of your chart known as the MC. This is a very sensitive area and it acts as a pointer, showing where your working abilities lie. Of course, other areas of your chart are also important (see pages 74–5). But when you look up the sign on your MC in this table, you may be in for a surprise!

SIGN	ON MC	STRENGTHENED BY
ARIES ♈	You are known for your innovation; being first; being a winner	Mars in Capricorn Mars in 10th house Saturn in Aries
TAURUS ♉	You're reliable and steady; you stick at what you've set out to do	Venus in Capricorn Saturn in Taurus Saturn in 2nd house
GEMINI ♊	A whizz kid; brainy, clever; interested in new ideas and fresh approaches to work	Mercury in Capricorn Mercury in 10th house Uranus in Gemini
CANCER ♋	Warm; maternal; emotional; prone to moodiness; tenacious; prickly	Moon in Capricorn Moon in 4th or 10th house
LEO ♌	Artistic and creative; a need to be in the spotlight; organized; the boss	Sun in Capricorn Sun in 10th house
VIRGO ♍	Disciplined; resourceful; an expert; an eye for detail; high standards	Mercury in Virgo Mercury in 6th house Saturn in 6th house
LIBRA ♎	Considerate; balanced; you want to be seen to be courteous and polite	Sun in Libra Venus in Libra Venus in 10th house
SCORPIO ♏	Motivated; emotional intensity; you want to be productive and successful	Sun in Scorpio Sun in 8th house Pluto in 10th house
SAGITTARIUS ♐	Enthusiastic; optimistic; enterprising; expansive ideas; can be outspoken	Sun in Sagittarius Jupiter in Sagittarius Jupiter in 10th house
CAPRICORN ♑	You want to be respected; serious-minded; conventional; reliable	Saturn in Capricorn Saturn in 10th house
AQUARIUS ♒	You want to be your own person; original; unique; iconoclastic; challenging	Uranus in Aquarius Uranus in 10th house Sun in Aquarius
PISCES ♓	Instinctive and guided by emotions; possibly several different careers or jobs	Moon in Pisces Neptune in 10th house

4

Money

Ah, money! It's something we all need, but we each have our own particular attitude towards it. For some, it's simply a means to an end and not important in its own right. For others, it's an essential part of life and we place tremendous importance on our material values. In this chapter we'll be looking at two planets on your horoscope that have a strong bearing on our attitude to money — not only how we feel about it, but also the way we spend it and what we spend it on.

Astrology and Money

In this chapter we're putting Venus and Pluto under the microscope, because both planets have an important bearing on our attitude to money. As you know by now, Venus rules enjoyment, among other things, so when it comes to finances it tells us what we enjoy spending our money on. Pluto's rulership is very different. It's all about the things we hide from ourselves but which need to come out into the open so we can deal with them. And that might include our spending habits! Pluto is also associated with big money (hence the word 'plutocrat', meaning someone whose wealth gives them power), so its position in your chart can be an indication of whether you'll be in the money.

Here's a quick run-through of the houses in terms of what we spend our money on. Look at your horoscope to see which houses are occupied by one or more planets, so you can see where your money might go.

When looking at your chart to learn about your finances, pay particular attention to the two money houses. These are the 2nd and the 8th.

Money by house

Status symbols,
power dressing,
dominant parent

Long journeys,
holidays, further
education

Hobbies, your
friends, groups
and societies

Shared
expenditure,
sex, anything
mysterious

Charity, the things
you keep secret

Other people, gifts,
legal matters

10 11 9
1 8
2 7
3 6
4 5

Yourself! Your appearance
in general

Your health,
diet, pets, clothes

Investments,
luxury items,
treats

Fun, children, creative
projects, gambling

Short journeys,
gadgets, reading
matter

Home and family,
nostalgia, less
dominant parent

Your Venus Sign and Your Financial Attitude

What do you enjoy spending money on? Your Venus sign will give you some clues, whether it's describing your attitude to money or the emotional reasons behind some of your purchases.

✦

To discover the sort of items you enjoy buying, or your emotional reasons for buying them, think of the objects and activities described by your Venus sign.

✦

SIGN	YOUR ATTITUDE TO MONEY	WHY YOU SPEND IT
ARIES ♈	Carefree; easy come, easy go; impulsive; generous; self-centred	Looking for excitement; boredom; spur of the moment; to set a new trend
TAURUS ♉	Cautious; money means physical security; can be too materialistic	You love indulging yourself; you want value for money; as an investment
GEMINI ♊	It's a passport to having fun; can easily turn a blind eye to financial problems	To be in the know; to acquire new ideas; to keep yourself amused
CANCER ♋	Money in the bank makes you feel safe; cautious; thrifty at times	For comfort; to feel happy; you enjoy being generous to loved ones
LEO ♌	You love splashing it around in dramatic ways; self-indulgent and lavish	You simply can't resist; you need to look good; you have standards to maintain
VIRGO ♍	Careful; prudent; you scrutinize your accounts; reluctant to accrue debts	You've done the research and it's the best deal; it will allay your anxieties
LIBRA ♎	You love having it but aren't good at keeping it; can be a spendthrift	To make others like and appreciate you; to give everyone a good time
SCORPIO ♏	Astute; shrewd; not willing to take risks; you can prosper from other people	You're looking for a deep emotional charge; you want to calm yourself down
SAGITTARIUS ♐	Enthusiastic; optimistic; it's there to be used; not good at the detail	It's far too tempting to resist; it makes you feel good; idealism
CAPRICORN ♑	Careful; sensible; can be penny-pinching; money brings status and respect	You need to look the part; you need emotional reassurance; it's a good deal
AQUARIUS ♒	It's a means to an enjoyable end; you'd rather be happy than rich; philanthropic	You love making others feel good; you're fascinated by the subject matter
PISCES ♓	You trust your instincts; kind and generous; you can be a soft touch	You follow your gut instincts; it's a chance to escape from everyday life

Venus in the Twelve Houses

The house occupied by your Venus
describes the areas of life that
give you pleasure or
are rewarding for
other reasons.

**WHAT YOU SPEND
YOUR MONEY ON**
The essentials; items that
are made to last; status
symbols; impressing others

**WHAT YOU SPEND
YOUR MONEY ON**
Your friends; groups
and societies;
interesting books;
technology and
gadgets

EMPHASIZED BY
Venus in Capricorn
Saturn in 2nd house

EMPHASIZED BY
Venus in Aquarius
Uranus in 2nd house

**WHAT YOU SPEND
YOUR MONEY ON**
Perfumes; aromatherapy
oils; creative and artistic
pursuits; the cinema

EMPHASIZED BY
Venus in Pisces
Neptune in 2nd house

EMPHASIZED BY
Venus in Aries
Sun in Aries
Sun in 1st house

**WHAT YOU SPEND
YOUR MONEY ON**
New gadgets;
motorbikes; cars;
items just for you;
hats; facial care

EMPHASIZED BY
Venus in Taurus
Moon in 2nd house

EMPHASIZED BY
Venus in Gemini
Mercury in Gemini
Mercury in 3rd house

**WHAT YOU SPEND
YOUR MONEY ON**
Property; luxurious items;
delicious food; beauty
treatments; music

**WHAT YOU SPEND
YOUR MONEY ON**
Siblings; short-distance
journeys; local shopping
trips; books, films

10
12 11
1
2
3

You can refer to this table to see how transiting Venus affects your spending habits as it moves through each house in your birth chart.

WHAT YOU SPEND YOUR MONEY ON
Your latest enthusiasm; travel; books; socializing; learning something new

WHAT YOU SPEND YOUR MONEY ON
Items that mean something to you; wine; stocks and shares; your sex life

EMPHASIZED BY
Venus in Sagittarius
Jupiter in Sagittarius
Jupiter in 2nd house

EMPHASIZED BY
Venus in Scorpio
Pluto in 8th house

WHAT YOU SPEND YOUR MONEY ON
Your beloved; looking well groomed; extravagant treats; romantic restaurants

EMPHASIZED BY
Venus in Libra
Sun in Libra
Sun in 7th house

EMPHASIZED BY
Venus in Virgo
Mercury in Virgo
Mercury in 6th house

WHAT YOU SPEND YOUR MONEY ON
Small and delicate items; your health; making your life run smoothly; your pets

EMPHASIZED BY
Venus in Leo
Sun in Leo
Sun in 5th house

EMPHASIZED BY
Venus in Cancer
Moon in 4th house

WHAT YOU SPEND YOUR MONEY ON
Luxury goods and clothes; eating out; friends and family; children; theatre

WHAT YOU SPEND YOUR MONEY ON
Items for your home or family; comfort food; objects that you collect

Aspects of Venus –
Your Money and Possessions

Study your chart to see if Venus
makes any aspects to other planets
or the angles. You have already discovered
what Venus aspects say about you
romantically on pages 50–51, but here
you can see how they affect your
attitude to money and possessions.

If transiting Venus (the current Venus, not the one
in your birth chart) is making an aspect to one of your
natal planets, you can use this chart to discover how it
will affect you financially, because the themes are
the same for natal and predictive work.

VENUS ASPECT	INFLUENCE	STRENGTHENED BY
☉ SUN	You enjoy spending money on loved ones; you buy arty or creative items	Venus in Leo Venus in 5th house Sun in 2nd house
☽ MOON	You can't resist luxury; you adore giving presents; you can be quite materialistic	Venus in Cancer Venus in 4th house Moon in Taurus
☿ MERCURY	You're drawn to items that stimulate your mind; your social life can be expensive	Venus in Gemini Venus in 3rd house Mercury in 2nd house
♂ MARS	Possessions can spark strong feelings; money can cause partnership rifts	Venus in Aries Venus in 1st house Mars in Taurus
♃ JUPITER	A huge urge to splurge; generous; extravagant; fun-loving; you adore travel	Venus in Sagittarius Venus in 9th house Jupiter in 2nd house
♄ SATURN	Careful with money; can prefer to save than spend; may marry for money	Venus in Capricorn Venus in 10th house Saturn in 2nd house
♅ URANUS	Attitude to money can be erratic; you like money for the freedom it can bring	Venus in Aquarius Venus in 11th house Uranus in 2nd house
♆ NEPTUNE	Generous; kind but can be gullible; you feel it's your duty to donate to charity	Venus in Pisces Venus in 12th house Neptune in 2nd house
♇ PLUTO	Money can be a source of satisfaction but also a way of controlling others	Venus in Scorpio Venus in 8th house Pluto in 2nd house
ASCENDANT DESCENDANT	You enjoy spending money on your personal appearance and on partners	Venus in Aries or Libra Venus in 1st or 7th house
MC/IC	You may be known for your financial status; attracted to status symbols	Venus in Cancer or Capricorn Venus in 4th or 10th house

Pluto in the Twelve Houses

Pluto's house in your natal chart will reveal
the area of life that could be financially
powerful for you. Pluto is the planet of
buried treasure, so some of this
information could come as a surprise!

FINANCIAL POWER
Big business; being top dog; leadership roles

EMPHASIZED BY
Pluto in Capricorn / Venus in 10th house

FINANCIAL POWER
Travel of the body or mind; religion; higher education

EMPHASIZED BY
Pluto in Sagittarius / Venus in 9th house

FINANCIAL POWER
Leading a group; friendships; ideals; computers

EMPHASIZED BY
Venus in Aquarius / Uranus in 8th house

FINANCIAL POWER
Close relationships; shared businesses; inheritances

EMPHASIZED BY
Pluto in Scorpio / Venus in 8th house

FINANCIAL POWER
Working in secret or alone; the oil business

EMPHASIZED BY
Venus in 8th house / Neptune in 8th house

FINANCIAL POWER
One-to-one relationships; negotiations; intermediary roles; the law

EMPHASIZED BY
Pluto in Libra / Venus in 7th house

FINANCIAL POWER
Personal matters

EMPHASIZED BY
Sun in Aries / Venus in 1st house

FINANCIAL POWER
Work; being of service; health-related matters

EMPHASIZED BY
Pluto in Virgo / Venus in 6th house

FINANCIAL POWER
Personal finances; possessions

EMPHASIZED BY
Venus in Taurus / Venus in 2nd house

FINANCIAL POWER
The media; siblings; short journeys; schools

EMPHASIZED BY
Venus in Gemini / Venus in 3rd house

FINANCIAL POWER
At home; family matters; the past

EMPHASIZED BY
Moon in Cancer / Venus in 4th house

FINANCIAL POWER
Your talents; being your true self; taking the lead

EMPHASIZED BY
Sun in Scorpio / Venus in 5th house

11 10 9 8 7 6 5 4 3 2 1

Aspects of Pluto – Your Money

Aspects from Neptune to Pluto aren't listed here because they affect entire generations and don't have a personal influence on us. If you do have one of these aspects in your chart, it will only affect you at a personal level if an angle or another planet plugs into it, such as the Sun making one aspect to your Pluto and another to your Neptune.

Pluto is the planet of transformation, so any aspect that it makes with a planet or angle in your chart can signify an area where your life will be transformed, and this includes your finances.

PLUTO ASPECT	INFLUENCE	STRENGTHENED BY
☉ SUN	Strong purpose and determination; you can go from being poor to being rich; money transforms you	Sun in Scorpio Sun in 8th house Pluto in 2nd house
☽ MOON	Money can give you power at home or with loved ones; wary of being conned	Moon in Scorpio Moon in 8th house Pluto in 4th house
☿ MERCURY	Great for thinking and talking about money; good for financial research	Mercury in Scorpio Mercury in 8th house Pluto in 3rd house
♀ VENUS	Money or emotions can be used for power; can do well on the stock market	Venus in Scorpio Venus in 8th house Pluto in 2nd house
♂ MARS	Finances can trigger angry outbursts; you will work hard for material gain	Mars in Scorpio Mars in 8th house Pluto in 8th house
♃ JUPITER	The potential to amass great wealth and power; avoid exploiting people	Jupiter in Scorpio Jupiter in 8th house Pluto in 9th house
♄ SATURN	You are careful with money and can worry about not having enough of it	Saturn in Scorpio Saturn in 8th house Pluto in 10th house
♅ URANUS	Your finances can be erratic; can make money from inventive ideas	Uranus in Scorpio Uranus in 8th house Pluto in 11th house
ASCENDANT DESCENDANT	You can become obsessive about your finances or the power they bring you	Pluto in 1st, 6th, 7th or 12th house
MC/IC	An ambition to be known for your financial situation; a drive for success	Pluto in 4th or 10th house

5

Friends and family

We've already looked at sexual and romantic partnerships in Chapter 2, so here we're going to examine other types of relationship, including friendships and family connections. As you'll discover, your horoscope has plenty to say about these, and with its help you'll be able to understand your own relationships better and possibly even find ways to improve them. Don't forget that you can also use this chapter to see how the people in your life relate to others. It could give you some brilliant clues about how to handle them better!

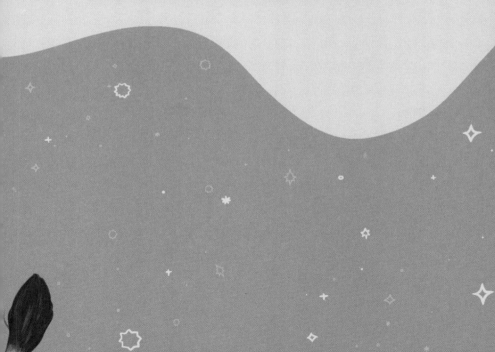

Your Horoscope and Relationships

In this chapter we're going to look at the roles that the planets play in relationships, because each one of them affects us in a different way. We're also going to examine the Moon in detail, as it describes what makes us feel comfortable. In addition, we'll be scrutinizing some of the relationship houses to discover the messages they have for us. Together, they cover every type of relationship, from families to friends, from colleagues to bosses, and much more besides.

Not every astrological house is connected with a specific relationship, but each of them describes something connected with partnerships. We'll be concentrating on three of these houses because they govern the relationships that most of us have and where we can sometimes struggle, despite our best efforts. These are our relationships with siblings and neighbours (3rd house); families (4th house); and friends (11th house).

If you want to understand how you behave in any other type of relationship, you need to do two things:

✳ Analyze any planet that falls in that house in your birth chart by combining the meaning of the planet with the meaning of the house.

✳ Analyze the way the sign on the cusp of that house affects you by combining the meaning of the sign with the meaning of the house.

You'll find all the information you need to do this in Chapter 1.

Relationships by house

People from other countries and cultures; religious figures

Older friends and relatives; people you respect; your boss; your dominant parent

Close, intimate and/or sexual relationships; taboo relationships

Friends; kindred spirits; groups and societies

One-to-one relationships; open enemies

Secret relationships; compassionate relationships; secret enemies

Colleagues; clients; customers; pets

How you regard and greet the outer world

Lovers; children; your favourite people

What you own, which can lead to possessiveness

Families; nephews and nieces; your less dominant parent

Siblings, cousins and neighbours

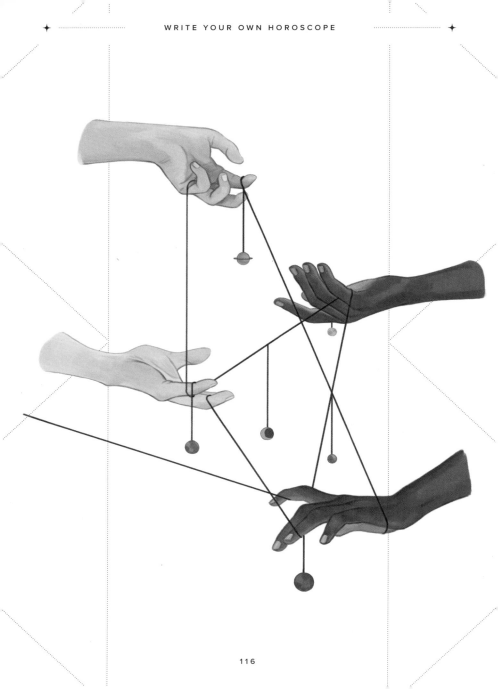

The Planets and Relationships

Every planet in the solar system has an effect on the way we connect with others. Venus, for example, has an obvious impact because it rules what we love and the way that we love it. Mars, of course, is the planet of sex and desire, as we discovered in Chapter 2. But both of them have a much broader impact than that. All the other planets also influence our relationships in many different ways, and it helps to think laterally when analyzing them astrologically. For example, someone whose chart shows that they are shy and have a tendency to be reclusive (such as an emphasis on Virgo, Capricorn or the 12th house) may enjoy close friendships but struggle when they're with groups of people.

On the other hand, someone who is easily angered and has a restless streak (look for an emphasis on Aries, Aquarius or a strong Mars and Uranus, possibly in aspect to each other) may have volatile relationships because they find it so difficult to stay on an even keel.

✦

Take your time when analyzing each planet in your chart and what it has to say about your relationships. Start simply and jot down all your thoughts. As you work, new ideas will come to you. Consider the areas of your relationships that you're happy with, and don't be afraid to consider the ones that could do with some work. After all, that's the best way to improve them!

✦

The Sun

Your Sun sign – also known as your star sign – speaks volumes about who you really are. It describes your essence and the journey you're taking through life. In terms of relationships, here are some of the areas it affects.

* What is most important to you
* Where and how you want to be noticed
* Your father and other father figures
* Where you gain your sense of identity
* Where you take the lead

The Moon

The Moon plays a major role in all our relationships because it has such a huge impact on our emotional reactions.

* Where you feel most comfortable
* Your instincts and gut feelings
* Your habits
* Your mother and other maternal figures
* What nurtures and feeds you emotionally
* Where you need to feel emotionally safe and secure
* How you mother others

Mercury

This describes the way you communicate with the rest of the world. Misunderstandings, lack of trust and downright lies can all fracture relationships, as can someone who talks so much that they never bother to listen to what anyone else says.

* What you think about
* What you talk about
* The way you talk to other people
* The way you listen to other people
* Siblings

♀ Venus

This is the planet of love. When interpreting its role in your birth chart, or in someone else's, don't forget that love comes in many forms.

* What you love
* How you show love
* What you need from others
* What makes you jealous or where you feel rivalry
* How you charm others

♂ Mars

It's the planet of sex but, as you can see, Mars is a lot more than that. All these facets of Mars can affect relationships.

* Your sexual urges and expressions
* What makes you angry
* How you express that anger and aggression
* What motivates you
* Your competitive spirit

♃ Jupiter

The planet of expansion and optimism brings enthusiasm and liveliness to our relationships.

* Your urge to expand and experience new things
* Your sense of adventure
* Optimism and positive thinking
* Your sense of humour
* Your generosity and warmth

ħ

Saturn

This heavyweight planet gives us structure and solidity. Without a strong Saturn, we can be unreliable in relationships or can struggle to settle down and make commitments.

* Your sense of responsibility
* What frightens you and dents your confidence
* What limits and restricts you
* How you can grow and mature
* Father figures

Uranus

Uranus likes to shake things up when they get stale, so it can be a much-needed influence in relationships, even though its action isn't always a comfortable experience.

* Your sense of innovation
* Your need for independence
* How you like to be different from everyone else
* Your urge for rebellion, shocking behaviour and wilfulness

When combining the meaning of a planet with its natal sign and the house it occupies, concentrate at first on very simple concepts so you don't get bogged down. For instance, when analyzing what the Moon in Leo in the 10th house means in terms of relationships, simply combine the key meanings of the Moon, Leo and the 10th house: your instinctive need (Moon) is to be admired and loved (Leo) by older friends or relatives (10th house).

Neptune

Neptune has a softening impact on us and is one of the planets of love. However, it can also cause confusion and mix-ups or emotional unreliability.

* Where your boundaries are weak or absent
* Your compassion and sensitivity
* Where and how you need to escape from life
* Romance and idealism

Pluto

Pluto can have a big impact on all our relationships because of its power and intensity. It can bring irrevocable change.

* What transforms you
* Sex and jealousy
* A need to control and manipulate situations
* What you suppress and try to bury emotionally

Bear in mind the nature of each planet, sign and house when interpreting them. Some are natural allies (such as Venus, Libra and the 7th house) and you can imagine them flowing well together. Others are less easy to interpret because their energies are so different. Uranus in Cancer in the 3rd house, for example, can be an uneasy clash between the Uranian urge for independence, the Cancerian need for emotional stability, and the busy, sociable nature of the 3rd house.

Your Moon Sign and Your Relationships

If you want to understand your emotional
needs and the way they affect your
relationships, you must pay close attention
to the Moon in your chart. Look up your
Moon sign to discover your needs, how
you mother and care for the people
in your life, and the areas of your personality
that need to be kept under control.

When analyzing your own Moon sign or that of someone
you know, think about how you can expand on the
information given here. How might someone with
the Moon in Cancer nurture others? Think of them
doing Cancerian things, such as cooking or
providing a cosy and safe environment.

Moon in Aries

EMOTIONAL NEEDS
To be *numero uno*; to take action;
to be independent

NURTURES BY
Rushing to someone's aid;
fighting their battles for them

CONTROL YOUR
Argumentative streak; childlike
need to come first; impetuosity

Moon in Taurus

EMOTIONAL NEEDS
Stability and security; to be
sensual; to be loved

NURTURES BY
Being loyal, loving and reliable;
being the provider

CONTROL YOUR
Possessiveness; distrust
of change; obstinacy

Moon in Gemini

EMOTIONAL NEEDS
Variety; to connect with others;
to be your own person

NURTURES BY
Listening; chatting; cheering
people up; keeping in touch

CONTROL YOUR
Talkative streak; wariness
of strong emotions

Moon in Cancer

EMOTIONAL NEEDS
To feel safe and cherished;
to feel that you belong

NURTURES BY
Mothering and feeding others;
being protective

CONTROL YOUR
Clinginess; moodiness;
defensiveness

Moon in Leo

EMOTIONAL NEEDS
To be in the limelight;
to excel at something

NURTURES BY
Showing love and generosity;
being loyal

CONTROL YOUR
Pride and ego; showiness;
need to be noticed

Moon in Virgo

EMOTIONAL NEEDS
To be busy; to help others;
to achieve things

NURTURES BY
Being useful; giving advice
and practical help

CONTROL YOUR
Worries; anxieties;
inability to fully relax and let go

Moon in Libra

EMOTIONAL NEEDS
Harmony and co-operation;
being with other people

NURTURES BY
Being considerate and courteous;
seeing others' points of view

CONTROL YOUR
Need to be a people-pleaser;
reluctance to face harsh reality

Moon in Scorpio

EMOTIONAL NEEDS
Intense and deep connections;
loyalty and affection

NURTURES BY
Intuitively knowing what others
need; being a confidante

CONTROL YOUR
Need to be in control;
suspicious nature

Moon in Sagittarius

EMOTIONAL NEEDS
Freedom; to explore the
world and fresh ideas

NURTURES BY
Being enthusiastic, positive
and fun-loving

CONTROL YOUR
Urge to roam; bluntness;
tendency to exaggerate

Moon in Capricorn

EMOTIONAL NEEDS
To be taken seriously;
to earn respect; to be strong

NURTURES BY
Being responsible and reliable;
providing a reality check if necessary

CONTROL YOUR
Pessimism; emotional reserve and
reticence; fear of being shut out

Moon in Aquarius

EMOTIONAL NEEDS
To do things in your own way;
to be independent

NURTURES BY
Giving a fresh take on situations;
by being original

CONTROL YOUR
Coolness; reliance on logic
rather than love; arrogance

Moon in Pisces

EMOTIONAL NEEDS
Sensitivity; love; kindness;
peace; a quiet life

NURTURES BY
Being compassionate and supportive;
doing your utmost to help

CONTROL YOUR
Escapist tendencies; naivety; reluctance
to deal with difficult situations

The Moon in the Twelve Houses

The house that your Moon occupies in your birth chart will describe the areas of life in which you feel most comfortable, and therefore where you connect with others most successfully.

RELATIONSHIP STYLE
Drawn to people you admire or who are successful; you may mother your boss

WATCH OUT FOR
Putting your working life and ambitions ahead of relationships

RELATIONSHIP STYLE
Friends feel like family; you enjoy being part of a group; kind and helpful

WATCH OUT FOR
Having so many friends that you wear yourself out

EMPHASIZED BY
Moon in Capricorn
Saturn in 4th house

RELATIONSHIP STYLE
Instinctive; intuitive; good at tuning into others at a deep level; humanitarian

WATCH OUT FOR
Not having enough time for yourself; being overwhelmed emotionally

EMPHASIZED BY
Moon in Aquarius
Uranus in 4th house

EMPHASIZED BY
Moon in Pisces
Neptune in 4th house

RELATIONSHIP STYLE
Great at attuning to others; responsive; sensitive; intuitive; considerate

WATCH OUT FOR
Soaking up other people's moods; taking on their problems

EMPHASIZED BY
Moon in Cancer or Pisces
Mars in Cancer

EMPHASIZED BY
Moon in Taurus
Venus in Cancer
Venus in 2nd house

RELATIONSHIP STYLE
Wary of change; a need for traditional relationships; warmly emotional

WATCH OUT FOR
Displays of possessiveness; playing it too safe emotionally

EMPHASIZED BY
Moon in Gemini
Mercury in Cancer

RELATIONSHIP STYLE
Bright; talkative; good at discussing problems; maternal towards siblings

WATCH OUT FOR
Talking too much and not listening enough; flightiness

10
11
12
1
2
3

RELATIONSHIP STYLE
People fascinate you; relationships with people from other countries and cultures

WATCH OUT FOR
Getting bored with someone when you get to know them

EMPHASIZED BY
Moon in Sagittarius
Jupiter in 9th house

RELATIONSHIP STYLE
You need to create strong and deep emotional connections

WATCH OUT FOR
Creating too much emotional intensity; jealousy

EMPHASIZED BY
Moon in Scorpio
Pluto in 8th house

RELATIONSHIP STYLE
A strong maternal streak; may get on better with women than with men

WATCH OUT FOR
Being so closely connected to others that you mirror them

EMPHASIZED BY
Moon in Libra
Venus in 4th house

EMPHASIZED BY
Moon in Virgo
Mercury in 6th house

RELATIONSHIP STYLE
Cautious; you enjoy being looked after or looking after others; a good colleague

WATCH OUT FOR
Allowing others to be too reliant on you; worrying about others

EMPHASIZED BY
Moon in Leo
Sun in 4th house

RELATIONSHIP STYLE
Playful and great fun; particularly good with children; drawn to creative people

WATCH OUT FOR
Can think that you know best; behaving like a parent to lovers, not an equal

EMPHASIZED BY
Moon in Cancer

RELATIONSHIP STYLE
Protective; caring; loving; focused on your family; a born home-maker

WATCH OUT FOR
Being too clingy; smother love; being suspicious of outsiders

9 8 7 6 5 4

Aspects of the Moon –
Your Relationships

Studying the aspects that your natal
Moon makes will give you extra insight
into the way it operates in your chart.

Don't forget that you can use these tables to understand
someone important to you, such as a friend or colleague.
Look at their birth chart to see which aspects their Moon
makes. This may help you to appreciate them more fully.

MOON ASPECT	INFLUENCE	STRENGTHENED BY
☉ SUN	Popular; good social life; sometimes an inner lack of harmony translates into relationship difficulties	Sun in Cancer Sun in 4th or 5th house Moon in Leo Moon in 5th house
☿ MERCURY	People love the way they can talk to you; you're clever and quick-witted; understanding and kind	Mercury in Cancer Mercury in 4th house Moon in Gemini Moon in 3rd house
♀ VENUS	Loving, warm and considerate; a need for pleasant relationships and to avoid strife and rows	Venus in Cancer Venus in 4th house Moon in Taurus or Libra Moon in 2nd or 7th house
♂ MARS	You're a real live wire; can be too honest and direct; can be argumentative and defensive	Mars in Cancer Mars in 4th house Moon in Aries or Scorpio Moon in 1st house
♃ JUPITER	Expansive; enthusiastic; easy-going; you love being the generous host; can get things out of proportion	Jupiter in Cancer Jupiter in 4th house Moon in Sagittarius Moon in 9th house
♄ SATURN	Emotionally low-key and withdrawn; can find it hard to trust people; strong need for emotional security	Saturn in Cancer Saturn in 4th house Moon in Capricorn Moon in 10th house
♅ URANUS	Emotions are up and down; moody; can be detached and distant; you value your friends; may live alone	Uranus in Cancer Uranus in 4th house Moon in Aquarius Moon in 11th house
♆ NEPTUNE	Empathy and compassion; intuitive; can be escapist to avoid problems; may try to rescue others	Neptune in 4th house Moon in Pisces Moon in 12th house
♇ PLUTO	Intense emotional life, with a yearning for deep bonds with others; a strong need for privacy	Pluto in 4th house Moon in Scorpio Moon in 8th house
ASCENDANT DESCENDANT	You wear your heart on your sleeve; can be very dependent on others; close to your mother	Moon in Cancer or Libra
MC/IC	Strongly affected by your childhood, especially if it was unsettled; a need for secure relationships	Moon in Cancer or Capricorn

The 3rd House

This is the house that rules many of the people we know well – our brothers and sisters, stepbrothers and stepsisters, cousins and neighbours. It also rules other people that we see regularly, such as fellow commuters, as well as contacts we've made through social media. When analyzing the 3rd house of your birth chart, the first thing to do is to see if it contains any planets. If a planet is in the 2nd house but it lies less than 4 degrees from the cusp of the 3rd, try interpreting it as if it is in the 3rd. After all, it might be there if you used a different house system. If the 3rd house doesn't contain any planets, note the sign on its cusp and interpret that using the knowledge you've acquired about that sign. Refer back to Chapter 1 if you need help.

You can use this information when working out what to expect in relationships when a planet transits your natal 3rd house.

PLANETS IN THE 3RD HOUSE

Find out how each planet affects you if it occupies the 3rd house of your birth chart.

☉	**THE SUN**	Bossy; you want to be in charge; you enjoy planning social events
☽	**THE MOON**	Motherly; you provide the food and TLC; a sibling may need help
☿	**MERCURY**	Chatty; you like to keep in touch with everyone; younger siblings
♀	**VENUS**	Tactful; you're the go-between who keeps things on an even keel
♂	**MARS**	Dynamic; sibling rivalry; you can enjoy sparring with others
♃	**JUPITER**	Fascinated by others; relationships teach you a lot; far-flung siblings
♄	**SATURN**	Cautious; you worry about everyone; siblings can be older than you
♅	**URANUS**	Idiosyncratic; you can take pride in not quite fitting in; estranged or adopted siblings
♆	**NEPTUNE**	Sensitive; you tune into undercurrents; there can be secrets about siblings
♇	**PLUTO**	Powerful; you create intense connections with others

The 4th House

If you want to understand how you fit into your family and home life, this is the house to study when you look at your birth chart. It rules everything that's familiar to us, so it's a very important house for most of us. In terms of relationships, it governs the people we feel at home with, such as those we live with. It also rules our less dominant parent.

As with all the houses, you need to see if the 4th house of your birth chart contains any planets, so you can read about them here. Don't forget to include any planets that are very close to the end of the 3rd house because they can give you extra information. You can also look at the sign on the cusp of the 4th house and analyze that.

A parent will still be described in a birth chart even if you are no longer in contact with them for some reason. They may not be in your life but they are definitely in your chart.

PLANETS IN THE 4TH HOUSE

What does it mean if you have one or more planets in the 4th house?
Here is your answer.

☉	**THE SUN**	You enjoy attention; you like to make the decisions
☽	**THE MOON**	Caring; sentimental; a big focus on mother figures
☿	**MERCURY**	Home is a good place for discussions and reading
♀	**VENUS**	You need to be in beautiful surroundings; you don't like family discord
♂	**MARS**	There can be lots of arguments and a desire to compete with each other
♃	**JUPITER**	You get on well with everyone; a home with plenty of laughter
♄	**SATURN**	Restrained with family; a strict parent or family background
♅	**URANUS**	You may prefer to live alone; you can be the family scapegoat
♆	**NEPTUNE**	Compassionate; a parent may be a martyr or is absent
♇	**PLUTO**	Intense emotions; can be a taboo connected with the family

The 11th House

This is the house of friends, groups and other people who are on the same wavelength as you. Any planets in this house will describe the type of friends you like and the sort of friend you are. Don't panic if you don't have any planets here. It doesn't mean you don't have any friends! If there is a planet at the very end of the 10th house, you can include it in the 11th house. And if there is no planet there either, simply look at the sign on the cusp of the 11th house in your birth chart, combine it with the meanings of the 11th house, and you will understand how that house operates for you.

PLANETS IN THE 11TH HOUSE

Here are the meanings of planets in the 11th house.

☉	**THE SUN**	You love being part of the gang, and you may be the leader, too
☽	**THE MOON**	Friends feel like family; you love belonging to different groups
☿	**MERCURY**	Plenty of conversation, especially on intellectual topics
♀	**VENUS**	You have lots of friends but there can be rivalry between you
♂	**MARS**	Friends can become lovers or vice versa; happy to help friends
♃	**JUPITER**	Expansive, generous and popular; may go travelling with friends
♄	**SATURN**	Generation gap between friends; serious and responsible
♅	**URANUS**	You're drawn to unusual friends; you like keeping your independence
♆	**NEPTUNE**	You're kind to friends but can be too idealistic and gullible about them
♇	**PLUTO**	A select group of friends; transformative and/or intense friendships

The MC and IC

These two angles have plenty to say about your family background. A planet conjunct the MC or IC has a powerful influence on your childhood, upbringing and domestic life, as does a planet that forms any other aspect to one or both of these angles. Don't worry if no planets aspect this axis because the sign of the MC and the sign of the IC will give you plenty of information about your childhood, parents and your home life.

THE MC

In many house systems this angle forms the cusp of the 10th house. Although the MC is most commonly associated with ambition and what you are aiming for in life, as well as how you are regarded by others, it also has connections with your parents and, in particular, the parent who has had the most impact on you. The sign on the MC will reveal plenty of information about this parent. Capricorn on the MC, for instance, might describe a parent who is strict, conventional, rather chilly emotionally and who has taught you to learn to fend for yourself. Pisces on the MC is very different, describing a parent who has Piscean attributes. They might be kind and sensitive, indecisive or may not have been there (either literally or metaphorically) while you were growing up. They might even work in the Navy, with boats or on the sea.

THE IC

This angle describes your early life, including your childhood and the atmosphere in which you grew up. It is also descriptive of the parent who had less of an impact on you. The same rules for interpretation apply here as for the MC, so look at the sign on the IC and then consider what it reveals.

Aquarius on the IC might describe a parent who was brilliant, quick and clever. They probably weren't very demonstrative or openly affectionate, but they encouraged you to think for yourself and to be independent from an early age. You may have moved house several times while you were growing up (Aquarius can be a restless sign). By contrast, Cancer on the IC could describe a parent who was strongly protective of you, perhaps to the point of you feeling slightly stifled or trapped. They may have given you a safe and traditional childhood, with an emphasis on family ties and a nostalgic view of the world. Food may have played an important part in family life.

The IC is a very sensitive part of the chart, so be particularly careful if you're interpreting the IC in someone else's chart. Try to interpret it objectively, and don't make judgements about the other person's parents or family background. Simply describe what you think their IC is saying, while being open to the idea that you may not have got it quite right. After all, astrology is an art!

6

Your potential – who could you be?

Your horoscope is like a map of your life. It shows all sorts of paths for you, some of which you have probably already discovered for yourself. But there are other avenues waiting for you that you may never have considered, and that's where astrology can be so exciting. Use it to analyze the promise and potential in your chart, so you can explore new areas of life and find fresh ways to use the talents you already know you have, as well as discover all sorts of gifts that are only just being revealed to you.

Finding Out Who You Are

We all express our potential in different ways. One person might turn a talent into a successful career. Another may enjoy exploring some of their gifts in their spare time, in voluntary work, or simply by doing something they love whenever they get the chance. The list of gifts and talents available to us all is infinite, whether we focus on those that are incredibly creative or deeply practical. After all, being able to saw a piece of wood in a perfectly straight line requires just as much talent as being able to do the splits or paint a portrait. So the ideas in this chapter are intended to be hints and prompts for your imagination.

PUTTING THE PIECES TOGETHER

When assessing your own horoscope, think about the central meanings of each planet, sign and house, and then consider the messages they might carry about your potential and the areas of life waiting to be explored. Remember that these possibilities can cover spare-time activities as well as careers and relationships, and all sorts of other things as well. It's essential to bear in mind that there are many ways of expressing the same combination of planet, sign and house position. Having Mercury in Cancer in the 10th house might mean being well-known (10th house) for writing (Mercury) about family matters or history (Cancer), or it could indicate building a business (10th house) involving small plants (Mercury) grown for food (Cancer). Use your imagination to come up with possible combinations in your own chart, and see if they appeal to you.

LOOKING AT THE ELEMENTS

Don't forget to consider the balance of elements in your chart because this will show where your natural skills lie. Having the majority of planets in one element acts like a pointer, showing the activities and areas where you blend in perfectly. If you have a good mix of elements it means you have more choice. Equally, if you don't have any planets in an element, you may be strongly drawn to it as a compensation for this lack.

Fire

This can be literally doing things that involve fire, such as working in the fire service, installing or selling wood-burners, having bonfires or teaching yourself how to flambé the perfect steak. Alternatively, you might express the fire element by being enthusiastic, encouraging others or always doing things quickly.

Earth

Literal examples include working with the land, estate agency, forest bathing or being a locksmith (earth wants security). More general examples include providing stability for others and for yourself, or being grounded and dealing with the facts.

Air

Among the literal expressions are sky-diving, being a pilot, learning about clouds, studying astronomy or campaigning for cleaner air. Abstract examples include writing, working on a phone helpline and teaching yourself something new.

Water

Maybe you feel drawn to oceanography, hydrotherapy, becoming a plumber, swimming, surfing or creating a pond. You might also show compassion and understanding, or have a very strong intuition that guides you through life.

Looking at the Signs

Here, we're concentrating on the twelve signs of the zodiac. Each one rules a whole host of different things, including precious stones, colours, metals and all sorts of objects, some of which are more obvious than others. They are areas of potential for you to explore further.

If you want to discover the hidden potential in your own chart, you can start small, using the astrological knowledge you've already acquired. You can then branch out and become inventive, thinking up some of the things and people that each sign, planet and house represent. This is not only a good astrological exercise but might also give you some great ideas about how to use the potential in your chart.

♈ ARIES

The brain
The army
Iron
Surgery
Tools
Diamonds
Hairdressers
Red
Manufacturing
Sheep

♉ TAURUS

Banking
Money
The neck and throat
Dancing
Green
Jewellery
Emeralds
Pianos
Copper
Cattle

♊ GEMINI

Siblings
Hands, arms and lungs
Magazines
Public transport
Schools
Yellow
Quicksilver/mercury
Telephones
Agate
Monkeys

♋ CANCER

Food
Silver
Silvery colours
Pearls
Home life
Breasts and the stomach
Glassware
The sea
Crabs
Pubs

♌
LEO
Gold
The heart and spine
Orange
Gambling
The theatre
Pleasure
Golf courses
Parties
Sports
Felines

♍
VIRGO
Quicksilver/mercury
Brown
The nervous system
and bowels
Cafés
First aid
Healing
Maps
Diet and nutrition
Sewing
Bees

♎
LIBRA
Beauty parlours
Interior design
Furniture
Blue
The kidneys
Sapphires
Copper
Cosmetics
Social functions
Tailors

♏
SCORPIO
Crimson
Red wine
Topaz
Snakes and reptiles
Taxation
Sex organs
Witchcraft
Sarcasm
Psychiatry
Iron

♐

SAGITTARIUS

Purple
Faiths and beliefs
Turquoise
Further education
Horses
International matters
Law courts
Tin
Publishing
The hips and thighs

♑

CAPRICORN

Carpenters
Goats
Grey
Lead
Government officials
Old age
Bones, teeth and skin
Mountains
Carnelian
Politicians

♒

AQUARIUS

Ultramarine
The calves, shins
and ankles
Astrology
Science and technology
Inventions
Computers
Electricity
Revolutions
Lead
Television

♓

PISCES

Institutions
Aquamarine
Watercolours
Dancing
The feet
Fish
The Navy
Perfume
Sleep
Amethyst

Looking at the Planets

Each of the planets has an area of rulership too. You will see some overlap between a planet and the sign/s that it rules, but you'll also see some interesting differences.

The lists here are only a tiny selection of the objects and situations ruled by each planet. You can expand on them yourself by reflecting on the nature of a particular planet, such as the Moon ruling our habits and what we find familiar, and then thinking about what else might come under that planet's influence.

THE SUN

Lions and cats
Entertainment
Marigolds
Leaders and heads of state
Royalty
The ego
Heat
Enjoyment
Creativity
Citrus fruits

THE MOON

Memory
Dreams
The sea and tides
Liquids
The public
Restaurants
Kitchens
Ghosts
Pregnancy
Handbags

MERCURY

Methods of communication
News
Shops and merchandise
Negotiations
Small plants
Public speaking
Writing
Cars
Messengers
Accountancy

VENUS

Beds and bedrooms
Fashion
Finance
Engagements and marriages
Guests
Hotels
Jewellery
Music
Manners and courtesy
Presents

MARS

Ambition
Sharp objects
Engineering
Fireworks
Dangerous jobs
Guns
Soldiers
Boxing
Spicy and pungent foods
Heat

♃
JUPITER
Archery
Horses
Law courts
Places of worship
Universities and colleges
Exaggeration
Wealth
Laughter
Stocks and shares
Publishing

♄
SATURN
Agriculture
Architecture
Elderly people
Customs and traditions
Frozen places and things
Leather objects
Junk and thrift shops
Mountains
Lonely places
Osteopathy

♅
URANUS
Shocks and surprises
Lightning
Revolution and rebellion
Modernization
Eccentric people
Clubs and groups
Complementary therapies
Engineering
Computer technology
Outer space and astronomy

♆
NEPTUNE
Music
The cinema
Essential oils
Perfumes
Mysteries
Glassware
Fishing
Romance
Photography
Secret societies

♇
PLUTO
Dogs
The unconscious
Psychotherapy
Earthquakes
Psychic talents
Hidden treasure
Volcanoes
Things that scare us
Compost
Big business

Looking at the Houses

Just as the signs and planets rule all sorts of things, so do the houses. Here are some suggestions to get your imagination working about areas of potential in each of your twelve houses.

THE 1ST HOUSE

Your face
Your head
Your outer appearance
Your habits
Your manners
Your behaviour
Your mannerisms
Your clothes
Your personality
How you appear to others
Sunrises

THE 2ND HOUSE

Possessions
Debts
The things you value
Money
Wealth
Stocks and shares
Precious stones
Vocal cords
Vocal problems
The throat
Scarves
Necklaces
Neck ties

THE 3RD HOUSE

Taxi drivers
Neighbours
Siblings
Cousins
Short journeys
Cars
Schools
Elevators
Running
Writing

THE 4TH HOUSE

Endings in general
The end of life
The past
Houses and land
Old buildings
Public buildings
Inherited tendencies
Families
The weather
Souvenirs

THE 5TH HOUSE

Enterprises
Lotteries and raffles
Casinos
Nightclubs
Children
Love and romance
Parties
Picnics
Sensuous activities
Holidays

THE 6TH HOUSE

Pets
The medical profession
Complementary medicine
Cafés and restaurants
Textiles
The police
Being of service
Nutrition
Hygiene
Medicinal herbs

THE 7TH HOUSE

Marriage
Sweethearts
One-to-one relationships
Open enemies
Litigation
Agreements
Alliances
Business partners
Peace
Sunsets

THE 8TH HOUSE

Close relationships
Shared finances
Other people's money
Losses
Inheritances and legacies
Death
The afterlife
The occult
Reincarnation
Sex

You can use any combination of these lists of signs, planets and houses when forecasting your future. For instance, if transiting Jupiter enters a new house in your chart, you can find out possible ways that it might affect you by combining the meaning of Jupiter with that of the house it's moved into.

THE 9TH HOUSE

Further education
International matters
Long-distance travel
Religious faith
Foreign languages
Lawyers and juries
Publishing
Aliens
Philanthropy
Philosophy

THE 10TH HOUSE

Ambitions
Goals
Achievements
Career
Social status
Reputation
Government officials
Bureaucracy
Public life
Status symbols

THE 11TH HOUSE

Friends
Kindred spirits
Acquaintances
Stepchildren
Hopes and wishes
Long-term plans
Clubs
Groups and societies
Hobbies
Business income

THE 12TH HOUSE

Charity
Institutions
Seclusion
Meditation
Creative visualization
Escapism
Downfall
Martyrs and victims
Self-sacrifice
Drugs

You can also learn more about family and friends using a system called 'derived houses'. For instance, if you want to know about your partner's boss, you'll find the information by counting 10 houses (bosses are ruled by the 10th house) from the 7th house (partners). Count anti-clockwise round the chart, starting at the 7th house. This will take you to the 4th house.

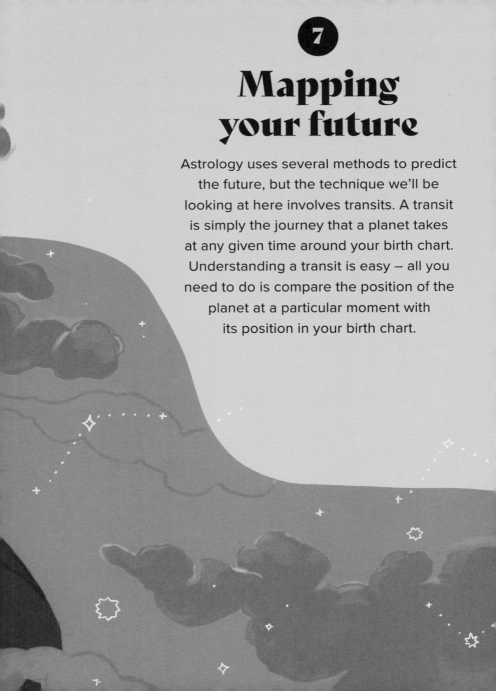

7

Mapping your future

Astrology uses several methods to predict the future, but the technique we'll be looking at here involves transits. A transit is simply the journey that a planet takes at any given time around your birth chart. Understanding a transit is easy — all you need to do is compare the position of the planet at a particular moment with its position in your birth chart.

Transits

From your vantage point on Earth, each planet, from the Sun to Pluto, is continually travelling around your horoscope. As it does so, the planet moves through each of your twelve houses in turn and, every now and then, makes an aspect to a natal planet or angle. Even when the planet isn't aspecting your natal chart, it will still have an impact through the house it's transiting. For instance, a planet transiting your 4th house will affect your home and family life.

Although transits are most commonly used to forecast the future, you can also delve into the past to see which transits were operating at a specific time. This is fascinating if you want to understand what was happening for you astrologically at a significant moment in your life, such as when you got married or landed that fabulous new job.

Use an astrology website or your own computer program to calculate your transits for a specific time. You will see what's called a biwheel, with your natal chart at the centre, and the transiting planets arranged around it in the outer wheel so you can see how they relate to your natal chart. See an example of this on page 156.

WHAT TO EXPECT

Whenever a planet transits a house or aspects one of your natal planets or angles, you will feel its effects. Can you look forward to a good time or should you be prepared for problems ahead? This is where you need some astrological knowledge, whether you're simply interpreting the combination of the transiting planet and the house it's currently occupying in your chart, or you're analyzing the aspect that the planet is making to your natal chart. The combination of the particular planets and angles involved, their signs, and the type of aspect they're forming will tell you what to expect. As with so many other things in life, transits are rarely all good or all bad. They often involve a mixture of experiences, with some that are positive and others that you may be less happy about.

Transits to natal planets or angles don't always occur independently of one another – for example, if the natal planet or angle that's being transited is in aspect to other planets in the birth chart. This sets off a chain reaction in the chart, with several areas being affected by one transit. Life can get really interesting when this happens! Alternatively, more than one transiting planet may be aspecting the same natal planet or angle, such as transiting Jupiter in Aquarius and Venus in Gemini both making aspects to your natal Mars in Libra.

Another example of transits coinciding is if several transiting planets make aspects to the natal chart at the same time, such as transiting Pluto in Capricorn conjunct your natal Moon, transiting Mars in Aries trining your Leo Sun, and transiting Neptune in Pisces squaring your Gemini Venus. Each of these aspects must be interpreted individually in order to get a sense of how they will affect you.

When calculating the aspects that a transiting planet makes to a natal planet, allow the same orbs as you do for a natal chart.

David
Natal
Inner Ring
13 Dec 1975, Sat
7:30 PM UT +0:00
Eastbourne
Tropical
Campanus

Transits
Event
Outer ring
13 June 2019, Thu
2:06 PM BST -1:00
Taunton, United Kingdom
Tropical
Campanus

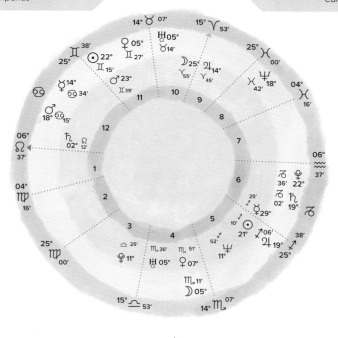

The planetary movements in the heavens reflect what's happening here on earth. Natal aspects and transits don't make things happen, yet there is a correlation between the positions of the planets and the events that take place at the time. This is often referred to as 'As above, so below'.

Life Cycles

When a transiting planet makes an aspect to its own natal position, it's not so much a transit as part of a bigger life cycle. This is especially true of Jupiter, Saturn, Uranus, Neptune and Pluto, because they move more slowly around your chart and therefore their effects are more significant.

MANY HAPPY RETURNS

When a transiting planet reaches a conjunction with its natal position in the chart, it's called a return, because it's returned to its original position. Planetary returns occur at set times in our lives, according to the length of that planet's cycle, and emphasize the areas of life ruled by that planet. There are also half-returns, when the transiting planet opposes its natal position. These, as well as quarter-returns, which are squares to the natal position, are used most commonly for the slower-moving planets of Jupiter to Pluto.

INTERPRETING A RETURN

A planetary return is the start of a new cycle for that planet, so it's the chance to assess what happened during the previous cycle and make plans that are related to the nature of the planet. A half-return can coincide with a challenge to the themes of the planet involved. It's our chance to assess the cycle so far, and it's also when we can reap the rewards of our hard work or when we need to make some important changes. We will look at solar and lunal returns on pages 180–3.

Return = the transiting planet making
a conjunction (0°) to its natal position

—

Half-return = the transiting planet making
an opposition (180°) to its natal position

Your Life's Path

When you work with planetary returns you'll begin to see how they coincide with significant periods in our lives. For instance, we all reach a major turning point when we're twenty-eight or twenty-nine, such as getting married or having children, around the time of our first Saturn return. As you will see, different planetary returns can coincide with different events.

7 YEARS	12 YEARS	14 YEARS	21 YEARS	24 YEARS
First Saturn quarter-return	**First Jupiter return**	**Saturn half-return**	**Second Saturn quarter-return**	**Second Jupiter return**
Going to junior school	Onset of puberty, growing up	Teenage problems, exams	Coming of age	Finding your way in the world

29 YEARS
**First
Saturn return**

Maturity,
responsibilities

36 YEARS
**Third
Jupiter return**

Something to
celebrate

42 YEARS
**Uranus
half-return**

Mid-life crisis, fresh
starts

45 YEARS
**Second Saturn
half-return**

Questioning your
life choices

48 YEARS
**Fourth
Jupiter return**

Looking for
meaning in life

60 YEARS
Fifth Jupiter return

Reaping the rewards
of your life

Second Saturn return

Taking stock of your life

72 YEARS
**Sixth
Jupiter return**

Making the
most of life

75 YEARS
**Third Saturn
half-return**

Adjusting
to old age

84 YEARS
Uranus return

Growing old disgracefully

Seventh Jupiter return

Looking for fresh
challenges

90 YEARS
**Third
Saturn return**

The wisdom
of old age

Retrogrades

If you want to forecast your future, you need to understand about retrograde planets. You may have already heard of Mercury retrogrades, when communications (one of the areas of life ruled by Mercury) can go haywire, but did you know that every planet, with the exception of the Sun and Moon, can go retrograde at some point during the year?

What is a retrograde planet?

When a planet is retrograde it's often described as moving backwards, because that's how it appears from our perspective on Earth. What's actually happening is that the planet has slowed down in relation to the Earth's orbit, so it seems to be going backwards until it speeds up again. During this time it goes through a series of phases:

* Stationary (appears to stop moving)
* Retrograde (appears to move backwards)
* Stationary (appears to stop moving again)
* Direct (starts moving forwards again)

A natal planet or angle is highlighted if a retrograde planet stations on it. It means you'll be dealing with something connected with that planet or angle that involves the themes of the stationary planet.

Retrogrades are opportunities for reflection, when we can reconsider, review and generally take stock of whatever is ruled by the planet and sign in question. So Mercury retrograde is a time for rethinking (Mercury rules our thoughts) whatever we're currently involved in, whereas Venus retrograde is an opportunity to review our values and the things we enjoy. New information can come to light during a retrograde phase, informing the decisions that we'll make when the planet goes direct. It's never a good idea to make decisions connected with the planet in question when it's retrograde as we may not yet have all the facts.

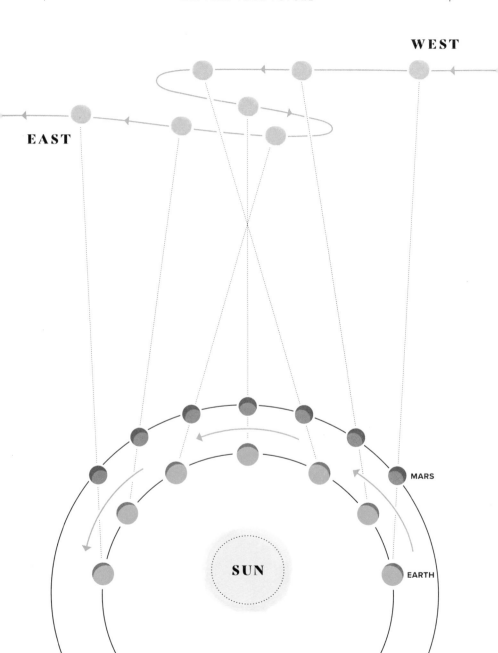

WEST

EAST

MARS

SUN

EARTH

Interpreting Transits

Find an astrology program online, or buy one, that will calculate your current transits. It will do this by comparing the position of the planets at the time of your choosing, with their position in your birth chart, using what's called a biwheel. Interpret each transit in turn, starting with Pluto and ending with the Sun. Ignore lunar transits because they're too fleeting for this sort of interpretation, unless you're looking at a specific day.

∗　Which house is the planet transiting? Interpret its effects.
∗　Is it aspecting any of your natal planets or angles?
∗　If so, refer to your interpretation of that natal planet or angle to see how it will react to the current transit.
∗　Is it going to station on one of your natal planets or angles, or aspect your chart while it's retrograde?

In each case, look for an affinity between the aspects being made by the transiting planet and the aspects made by that planet in your natal chart. For instance, if transiting Pluto is making an aspect to your natal Venus, and you have a Venus–Pluto aspect natally, you'll feel comfortable with these energies, so you might also respond to this transit instinctively rather than consciously.

Remember that each planet moves at a different speed. A Pluto transit could linger for months, whereas a Mercury transit will usually only last for a couple of days.

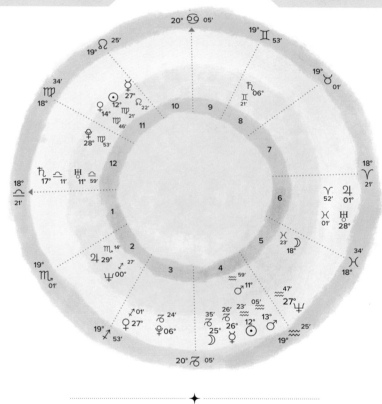

Amy
Natal
Inner Ring
5 Seot 1971, Sun
9:18 AM CDT +5:00
Birmingham, Alabama
Tropical
Campanus

Transits
Event
Outer ring
1 Feb 2011, Tue
8:50 AM CST +6:00
Birmingham, Alabama
Tropical
Campanus

Transits start to make their presence felt long before they become exact,
so you'll begin to notice them when they're about 5 or 6 degrees from exactitude.
Their influence will fade after they're exact, but you may still be dealing
with the fall-out of what was triggered at the time of the transit.

Mercury Transits

Mercury moves quickly and is never far from the Sun, so any transits it makes usually last for a relatively short time, unless, of course, it turns retrograde for a couple of weeks before moving forwards again. When this happens, it may aspect one of your natal planets or angles as it moves forwards, then again when it retrogrades, and then a third time when it moves direct again. This really emphasizes the need to think and talk about the area of life ruled by the natal planet.

When looking at Mercury's role in transits, you must bear in mind the following factors:

✳ Remember that Mercury is the planet of communication and thought, so the house position and sign of transiting Mercury shows what you'll be talking and thinking about.

✳ When transiting Mercury aspects a natal planet or angle, this is an opportunity to think, talk, write or generally communicate about whatever is represented by that planet or angle.

✳ Pay particular attention if Mercury is retrograde because the house it's transiting in your natal chart will be where you need to reflect, reconsider and revise your ideas, or perhaps reword something you've written.

✳ If transiting Mercury stations on one of your natal planets or angles, activities connected with this planet or angle may come to a brief halt so you are able to reconsider them.

✳ The aspect that transiting Mercury makes to a natal planet will be much stronger if that planet is transiting your natal Mercury. For instance, transiting Mercury squares your natal Mars and transiting Mars squares your natal Mercury.

Themes of a Mercury transit

Skills

Thoughts

Ideas

Short-distance travel

Communication

Themes of a Venus transit

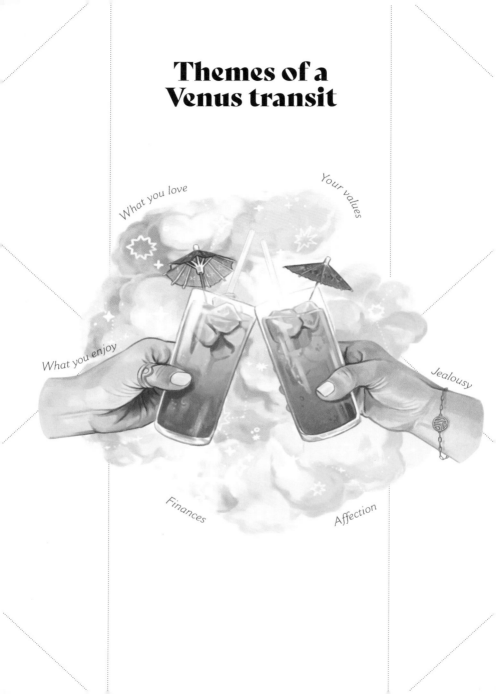

What you love

Your values

What you enjoy

Jealousy

Finances

Affection

Venus Transits

Just like Mercury, transiting Venus spends an average of one month in each house in your chart and completes its orbit roughly once a year. It can turn retrograde but this doesn't happen every year. When transiting Venus aspects a natal planet or angle, or simply moves through one of your natal houses, it indicates the area of your life that will be affected by Venusian themes.

* Venus transits bring a sociable and affectionate influence to whatever they contact in your natal chart. They show what you'll be enjoying and how you'll be doing it.

* Venus is passive and waits for good things to happen. Therefore, a Venus transit can be spent doing very little, so it might be an enjoyable break rather than a time of achievement.

* If transiting Venus goes retrograde, this is a chance to re-evaluate whatever Venus is highlighting by sign and house. Your feelings about it might change, or you may revise your priorities.

* Be wary of buying anything expensive or important during a Venus retrograde phase, in case you've changed your mind about it by the time Venus turns direct.

Mars Transits

We need energy to live, and Mars is the planet that supplies it. This means that the sign and house in your natal chart that's being transited by Mars at any given time is getting a huge burst of energy and motivation.

* Transiting Mars activates, energizes and motivates whatever it contacts in your natal chart, whether that's a planet, angle or house. This can be a busy time, with plenty going on. You may feel that everything connected with your natal placement has been speeded up, so you're often in a rush or you feel you're being chivvied along by others.

* Transiting Mars can act as a trigger for a long-term transit, such as one involving Neptune which can last for weeks or even months. When transiting Mars makes an aspect to one of the natal planets or angles involved in the long-term transit, or aspects that transiting planet (such as Neptune), it can set off events connected with that transit. You may only notice this when looking at a transit in retrospect.

Themes of a Mars transit

Drive

Anger

Sex

Initiative

Haste

Motivation

Competition

Aggression

Accidents

Confusing love with lust

Themes of a Jupiter transit

Optimism

Travel

Abundance

Enjoyment

The legal system

Expansion

Philosophy

Enlargement

Jupiter Transits

People often get very excited when they know they'll have a Jupiter transit because Jupiter has a reputation for bringing beneficial and enjoyable experiences. However, a Jupiter transit won't live up to expectations if we get our hopes up so high that reality comes as a disappointment.

* Jupiter spends roughly a year in each sign, so is the first of the slower-moving planets. Therefore, a Jupiter return is a significant event.

* Transiting Jupiter will expand and enhance whichever area of your natal chart it touches. This can sometimes manifest in physical ways, so transiting Jupiter conjunct your natal Moon might lead to a struggle with your weight, or Jupiter might transit your 4th house when you're thinking of expanding your home or family.

* Pay particular attention to the nature of the planet, angle or house being affected by a Jupiter transit. How will it react? For instance, Jupiter returning to its own position in your 2nd house of personal finances could indicate an extravagant time if other factors (such as Venus in the 2nd house) agree.

Saturn Transits

Whenever Saturn transits a part of your natal chart it tests the stability of what it finds there. No wonder Saturn transits have a reputation for bringing doom and gloom, although actually they're more often reality checks, bringing us down to earth and encouraging us to ensure that the areas in our lives being touched by Saturn are running smoothly.

* The good news is that a Saturn transit ultimately works to our benefit by getting rid of anything that isn't solid or long-lasting, so this can be replaced by something more worthwhile.

* A Saturn transit helps us to lay down solid foundations on which we can build — sometimes literally! It encourages us to develop a framework that can be developed and which will lead to better things.

* One complete Saturn cycle runs for just under thirty years. A Saturn return asks us to evaluate the stage we've reached in our lives, so we can either continue in the same vein or change tack. Ultimately, we are reminded of the tasks we still need to do but we also gain the rewards of all our hard work and effort so far.

Themes of a Saturn transit

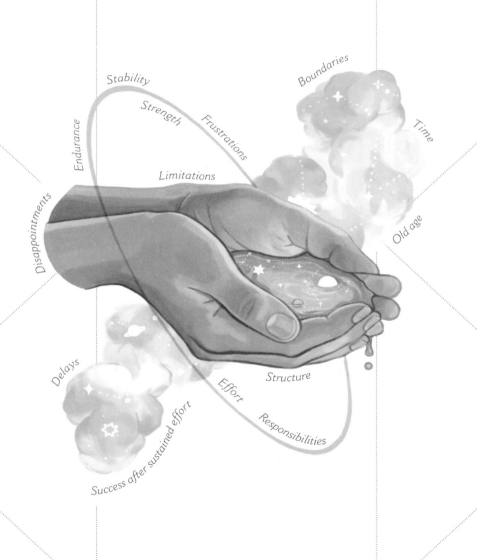

Stability

Strength

Frustrations

Boundaries

Endurance

Time

Limitations

Disappointments

Old age

Delays

Structure

Effort

Responsibilities

Success after sustained effort

Themes of a Uranus transit

Sudden events

Impulsive actions

Liberation

The unexpected

Originality

Revolution

Innovation

Controversy

Shock

Uranus Transits

Uranus likes to shake things up. It's the lawbreaker, the maverick, the experience you didn't see coming. Therefore, a Uranus transit brings surprises and unexpected events, but these have a greater purpose than simply leaving us open-mouthed with astonishment. Something new wants to break through during a Uranus transit. Maybe the old ways of doing things are no longer working and it's time for a fresh approach.

* Whenever transiting Uranus contacts a planet, angle or house in your natal chart, it livens it up. This can be exhilarating, when you never know what's round the corner and every day feels full of anticipation. Alternatively, a Uranus transit can be a time when it feels as though everything you've counted on is being swept away. Areas of life that you've been taking for granted or trying to ignore because you know they're not right suddenly become a source of shock or even disbelief. Something needs to change!

* Relationships that are affected by a Uranus transit can become fragmented. Someone you thought you really knew shows a different side of their personality, does something weird or deserts you. Or maybe you do one of these things or start to feel detached from the people you were previously close to. If a relationship starts under a Uranus transit it can be sudden, wildly exciting and dramatic, but it might end as quickly as it began.

Neptune Transits

A Neptune transit often operates at a very subtle level so it may not be nearly as noticeable as transits from other slow-moving planets.

* The natal house, planet or angle that's being transited by Neptune will experience Neptunian themes. Neptune clouds our sense of reality, distorting our view of life. Vague anxieties and fears can nag at us. Are they justified or merely figments of our imagination?

* Neptune transits can bring experiences of great spiritual or religious meaning. However, as with everything else connected with Neptune, we may not be seeing things as they really are, so might give ourselves a hard time for not being spiritual enough. Alternatively, we might think we've nailed it and it's everyone else who's got it wrong!

* Go slowly, check the facts and keep questioning yourself about the matters ruled by the natal planet or angle that's being transited by Neptune. This isn't the time to take your eye off the ball or just hope for the best, in case you miss something that needs your attention.

Themes of a Neptune transit

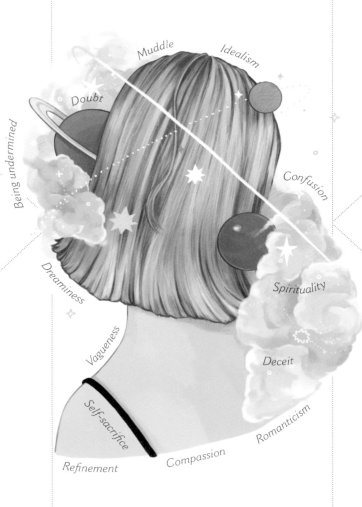

Themes of a Pluto transit

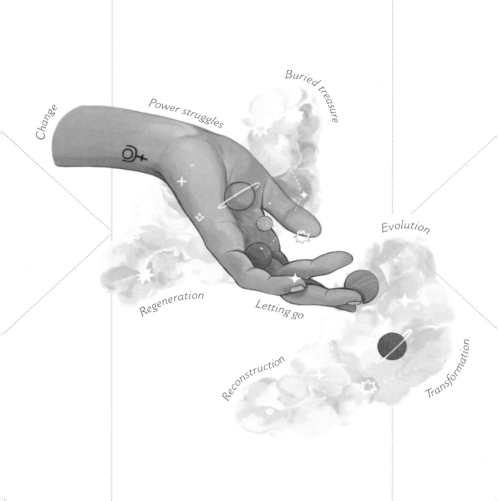

Change

Power struggles

Buried treasure

Evolution

Regeneration

Letting go

Reconstruction

Transformation

Pluto Transits

Pluto is the slowest-moving planet in the solar system, so a transit to a natal planet or angle can take weeks or even months to pass, and Pluto can spend years transiting a natal house. As a result, its influence becomes the psychic wallpaper of our lives, with occasional flare-ups of Plutonian activity when a faster-moving planet transits the area of the natal chart that's being affected by Pluto.

∗   Think of a Pluto transit as being a time of great transformation, whether on a physical, emotional or spiritual level. The old order is dying and something new is waiting to take its place. This can be a painful and frightening experience, especially if our fear of change has made us hold on to the things, people or situations that need to be altered. The more we cling on to them and try to control what's happening, the more difficult it will be to release what needs to pass out of our lives.

∗   The changes that Pluto brings can sound alarming, which is why it's useful to remember that just as garden waste can be rotted down to use as valuable compost that will feed the soil, so a Pluto transit will help us to transform the things that no longer serve us into something new that will enrich and change us. One of the main themes for Pluto is buried treasure, and a Pluto transit helps us to find this treasure within ourselves.

Solar Returns

One of the best ways to forecast your year ahead is to use what's called a solar return. This is a chart set for the moment the Sun returns to the exact degree and minute of its natal position, and you read it as though it's a birth chart for the coming year. You can either set a solar return for your birthplace or for where you are on your birthday. Any good astrology computer program will calculate it for you.

A solar return is the chart of your year ahead. When reading it, pay particular attention to the following factors:

* The house position of the Sun – this is your main area of focus for the year ahead and where you'll be putting most of your energy.

* Any aspects that the Sun makes to other planets – they are the main themes you'll be dealing with.

* The sign on the Ascendant – this is the way you'll view the world during the year ahead.

* The position of the planet that rules the Ascendant – this is a major focus for you in the coming year

Don't be surprised if your solar return is set for
either the day before your birthday or the day after.
The Sun sometimes enters a sign early, which means
it's running ahead of itself for a while, and sometimes
late, when it's slightly behind its normal schedule.

Lunar Returns

If you want to examine your emotions, moods, needs and behaviour over the coming month, a lunar return will give you plenty of insight. It's set for when the Moon returns to its natal position, to the exact degree and minute, for the month ahead. It's therefore a very short-lived chart.

These are the most important things to look at:

* The house position of the Moon – this is where you'll be putting your emotional energy during the coming month.

* Any aspects that the Moon makes to other planets or angles – these will affect the way you express your emotions.

* The sign on the Ascendant – this is how you'll be expressing your emotional needs.

* Compare the lunar return with your natal chart – if a natal lunar aspect is repeated in the lunar return, it's something you'll be dealing with during the life of the lunar return.

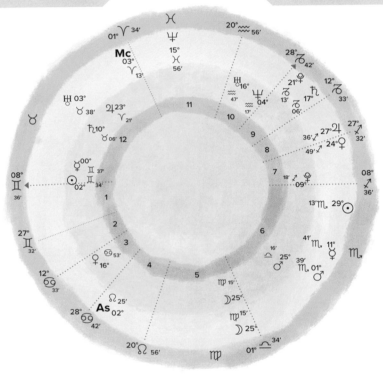

Jake
Natal
Inner Ring
24 May 1999, Mon
5:15 AM BST -1:00
Glasgow, United Kingdom
Tropical
Campanus

Jake
Lunar Return
Outer ring
21 Nov 2019, Thu
8:26:39 PM UT +0:00
Glasgow, United Kingdom
Tropical
Campanus

Set the lunar return either for your birthplace or
for the place you'll be on the day of the lunar return.
You can experiment with both to see which one
gives you the most accurate results.

Glossary

Ascendant The sign rising on the eastern horizon at the time for which the chart is calculated. It describes our physical appearance and the way we look at the world. The Ascendant, which is one of the angles of the chart, marks the cusp of the 12th and 1st houses.

Aspect The relationship between two planets, or a planet and an angle, when they are separated by a specific number of degrees.

Chart ruler The planet that rules the sign on the Ascendant. Its sign, house position and aspects expand the meaning of the Ascendant.

Cusp The division between the end of one sign or house and the start of the next.

Descendant The sign setting on the western horizon at the time for which the chart is calculated. It describes the way we engage with other people. The Descendant, which is one of the angles of the chart, marks the cusp of the 6th and 7th houses.

Direct motion The forward motion of a planet as viewed from our perspective on Earth.

Element Each sign belongs to, and is influenced by, one of the four elements: Fire (Aries, Leo and Sagittarius); Earth

(Taurus, Virgo and Capricorn); Air (Gemini, Libra and Aquarius); and Water (Cancer, Scorpio and Pisces).

Horoscope The name given to a natal chart and also the name given to an astrological forecast.

House One of the twelve sections of the chart, each of which rules a different area of life. They run anti-clockwise around the chart, starting on the eastern horizon.

House system A way of dividing up the chart into twelve houses or sections. House systems are many and varied, and choosing one is usually a matter of personal preference. The two featured in this book are Placidus and Campanus.

Imum Coeli (IC) In astronomy, it is the area directly below us at the time of our birth. It therefore represents our background, childhood and what feels familiar to us. The IC, which is one of the angles of the chart, marks the cusp of the 3rd and 4th houses in most house systems.

Midheaven (MC) In astronomy, it is the point above us at the time of our birth. It represents what we want to achieve and how we want to be regarded by others. The MC, which is one of the angles of the chart, marks the cusp of the 9th and 10th houses in most house systems.

Mode Each sign belongs to, and is influenced by, one of the three modes or qualities: Cardinal (Aries, Cancer, Libra and Capricorn); Fixed (Taurus, Leo, Scorpio and Aquarius); and Mutable (Gemini, Virgo, Sagittarius and Pisces).

Natal chart The chart calculated for the time and place of your birth.

Natal planet A planet in your birth chart. Its sign, degree, house and aspects in your chart describe how you express its energy in your life.

Orb The allowable number of degrees either side of exactitude for an aspect. For instance, two planets are in a trine aspect, which has an orb of 6°, when separated by between 114° and 126°.

Out of sign aspect An aspect that occurs between two planets, or a planet and an angle, that are not in their expected elements or modes for that aspect, such as a square between a planet at the end of Cancer and one at the start of Taurus.

Planetary ruler The planet that rules a particular sign.

Quadrant One of the four sections of the chart created by the crossing of the Ascendant–Descendant axis and the MC–IC axis.

Retrograde motion What appears to be the backwards motion of a planet as viewed from our perspective on Earth. It can be a very significant phase in forecasting work.

Return The moment when a planet returns to the exact position it occupies in the birth chart. A chart cast for this moment (a return chart) will describe the nature of that planet's cycle until its next return.

Stellium A conjunction of three or more planets. It is a concentration of planetary energy, so is always significant.

Transit The movement of a planet at any given moment and a very useful forecasting tool. When a transiting planet makes an aspect to a natal planet or angle, its energy activates the area of life represented by that planet or angle.

Unaspected planet Any planet that does not make any of the five main aspects to any other planet or angle. The unaspected planet's energy is independent of the rest of the chart and can be a driving force of the chart.

Resources

Online Chart Calculation

What's available on the Internet can change, of course, but here are some websites that offer free chart calculation at the time of writing.

Astro-Seek has a free chart calculator and lots of other information at https://horoscopes.astro-seek.com/birth-chart-horoscope-online

Astrology.com offers a free chart calculator at https://www.astrology.com.tr/birth-chart.asp

AstroDienst offers a free chart calculator and lots of other information at https://www.astro.com

Astrolabe has a free chart calculator at https://alabe.com/freechart/

The London School of Astrology has a free chart calculator and lots of other freebies at https://www.londonschoolofastrology.com/pages/freebies

Matrix Astrological Web Services offers a comprehensive online astrology program for which you pay a subscription at https://astrologysoftware.com/pro/wservices/web.html

Astrology Programs to Buy

Many companies, including the ones listed below, sell astrology calculation programs. Before buying, always check that they are suitable for your type of computer or phone, and also check the level of expertise required to use them, as some are more complex than others:

Astrograph astrology software at https://www.astrograph.com
AstroGold astrology software at https://www.astrogold.io
Matrix Software at https://astrologysoftware.com
Astrolabe at https://alabe.com

Books

There are so many astrology books to choose from, but these are helpful whether you're just starting out or want to deepen your astrological knowledge.

Cheung, Theresa, *The Astrology Fix*, White Lion Publishing, 2020
Hand, Robert, *Planets in Transit*, Para Research, 1976
Lundsted, Betty, *Transits*, Samuel Weiser, 1980
March, Marion, D. and McEvers, Joan, *The Only Way to … Learn Astrology, Volume III, Horoscope Analysis*, ACS Publications, 1982
Sasportas, Howard, *The Twelve Houses*, Flare Publications, 2007
Struthers, Jane, *Moonpower*, Eddison Books, 2017
Struthers, Jane, *Sun Signs*, Magpie Books, 2005
Stubbs, Janey, and Kirby, Babs, *Interpreting Solar and Lunar Returns*, Capall Bann Publishing, 2001
Tompkins, Sue, *The Consultant Astrologer's Handbook*, Flare Publications, 2006

Index

Acknowledgements

This book may carry my name on the cover but many people helped to make it a reality. Many thanks to everyone at White Lion Publishing, especially Zara Anvari and Michael Brunström for guiding the book through the publication process. As ever, grateful thanks and lots of love to my wonderful back-up team of my fabulous agent, Chelsey Fox, and my patient husband, William Martin. Many thanks also to AstroGold (https://www.astrogold.io), whose astrology program generated all the charts in the book.

First published in 2021
by White Lion Publishing,
an imprint of The Quarto Group.
The Old Brewery, 6 Blundell Street
London, N7 9BH,
United Kingdom
T (0)20 7700 6700
www.QuartoKnows.com

Text © 2021 Jane Struthers
Illustrations © 2021 Laura Medlicott

A catalogue record for this book is
available from the British Library.

ISBN 978-0-7112-5451-0
eISBN 978-0-7112-5452-7

10 9 8 7 6 5 4 3 2 1

Designed by Sarah Pyke
Printed in Singapore

About the author

Jane Struthers is a full-time professional astrologer and writer who has studied tarot, astrology and palmistry for over twenty-five years. She teaches astrology at the London School of Astrology, and has also lectured abroad on astrology and tarot. She writes the weekly astrology column for *Bella* magazine and is the author of thirty non-fiction books, including the best-selling *The Psychic's Bible* and *Red Sky at Night*.

MIX
Paper from
responsible sources
FSC® C016973